Ernest L. Norman
**Author, Philosopher, Poet, Scientist,
Director-Moderator of Unarius Science of Life**

UNARIUS
UNiversal **AR**ticulate **I**nterdimensional
Understanding of **S**cience

THE VOICE OF VENUS

The First Volume of

The Pulse of Creation Series

For information address:
The Unarius Educational Foundation, 145 S. Magnolia Avenue, El Cajon, CA 92020-4522

Library of Congress Cataloging-in-Publications Data:

Norman, Ernest L. 1904-1971
 The Voice of Venus Pulse of Creation Series, Vol. 1

   ISBN 0-932642-00-4 (alk. paper)
   ISBN 0-935097-33-3 (pbk. :alk. paper)

   1. Cosmology
   2. Extraterrestrial Civilizations
   3. Life After Death
   4. The Paranormal
   5. Continuity of Consciousness
   6. Life on Planet Venus
   7. Reincarnation

I. Title

Library of Congress Catalog Card Number 94-61990

*

CONTENTS

PREFACE

(Added January, 1961)

Any individual who has traced the course of written history has, no doubt been impressed not only with the great numbers of personalities who have illumined these historical pages but, in some instances, certain individuals were outstanding examples of their individual proclivities and talents. Any attempt to evaluate the author or his works on the basis of these past expressionists would be quite useless; particularly because the author is all-inclusive in his expression, and which runs the gamut in all known and some presently unknown factors and elements of life. Also, that these various works by the author are delivered in the scientific idiom of the twentieth century and contain nomenclature as expressionary elements which can be considered part of these sciences and in this respect are provable on the basis of their respective known physical sciences.

Moreover, the author has taken great pains and meticulous care in the preparation of these various expressions and in such construction and composition as to appeal to all classes and mental levels; and they can without difficulty be understood by either the layman or the physicist.

It would be well also, at this time, to mention an incontestable fact; that the author in his work is affiliated with one or more great Spiritual Organizations

1

which aid materially in various phases of delivery, such as preconditioning, spiritual healing, sleep teaching, etc. While these elements and Spiritual Organizations are still comparatively or completely unknown, this fact cannot be questioned. It must be remembered that the commonplace twentieth century electronic devices were not even dreamed of save by a few, fifty years or so ago. So it will be in the future. What the author has included in these various presentations may appear as fact to some, or fantasy to others. This has always been the customary reaction of man's evolutionary pattern and, should the doubters of today live but a few more decades, they could well see the fulfillment and complete justification in common knowledge and usage of what now appears to be an apparent fantasy of the day.

Even more than this, however, are other incontestable facts, thousands of them, written by an equal number of people who have had wonderful and sometimes miraculous healings and changes occur in their lives after they began studying these many works and lessons, some of which equal or excel various Biblical depictions of miracles; inasmuch as no physical contact was made and, other than the correspondence with these people, they had no contact with the author, as all correspondence is handled by his wife, Ruth. More remarkable in many instances, he did not even receive personal communications or notifications from some of these people until they were well on their way to recovery; and which fact, in itself, proves the existence of a vast Spiritual Organization and which, with the aid of the Higher, or Overself of the Author, Ernest L. Norman, had already entered into the reconstruction work before the lower, physical self was aware.

In this respect it can be said, that as a fourth

dimensional concept, space and time have been set aside in respect to instituting and completing a perfect concept of healing with some individual who has, through the ages of time in his many earth lives, been prepared and conditioned for this advent.

So far as Dr. Norman's personal life is concerned, there is to the casual observer, no reason to suspect that here is a person with a vast and infinite understanding of life and that he can, at any moment —just as he has done many countless thousands of times—transcend all known barriers of time and space, go into the past or future, talk fluently on all known aspects of life and, even though he has an incomplete formal education, is equally conversant with the physicist, the astronomer, the philosopher, the doctor or the nuclear scientist. While this has caused many learned savants, as well as many other people to be dumbfounded and amazed, yet he, in himself, is a very modest and unpretentious individual, dresses and lives simply and shuns public life.

His one crusade—if it can be called such—is to convince his fellowman that he, also, can do likewise and that such unusual mental faculties as mind reading mental telepathy, clairvoyance, the association of the past and future in the immediate present, is all a part of a proper mind function, acquired by any individual who can throw off the shackles of his limited material life and begin to make a progressive evolution into the future.

It should also be noted at this time that he (the author), is very careful to not make statements which he cannot prove; and should some good end be served, he stands ready to demonstrate the unlimited faculties of a properly trained mind. In some twenty years of research, practice and preparation, Dr. Norman demonstrated his abilities to many thousands of people. This was done in churches, cafes, taverns, on streets, in stores; even while dancing in public dance halls, he described intimate objects, loved ones, environments and surrounding conditions sometimes miles or continents away, quoting names and accurate physical descriptions to total strangers concerning their loved ones. He gave them accurate descriptions of past, present and future happenings in their lives. In a few instances he foretold death, its exact date, manner of happening, three or more years in advance.

To try to enumerate even a small fraction of these amazing demonstrations which were performed through these years would be quite impossible as it was carried on continuously, twelve or more hours a day and every day of these many years. Even in places where he earned his livelihood, from time to time, so far as the proprietor and personnel were concerned, they were also benefited. In fact, all people with whom he came in contact had wonderful healings and adjustments take place in their lives; yet this was done quietly, so much so that, in many instances, many of these people were not even aware that a miracle had occurred. Their consciousness in this respect assumed a natural and non-reactive attitude in the course of this event. To others, however, their personal experience was a great and wonderful happening, still remembered and talked about should occasion arise.

On the day he was born there was, to his parents at least, one indication that he was an unusual child; although his body was of normal size, he had the large and fully developed head of an adult and even at the tender age of three years, a hat could not be put upon his head which was less than an over-size seven and one-half. Before that time, he had already taught himself to read and write. At the age of five he constructed his first microscope. This was done by unscrewing the first eye section draw tube of his father's telescope and, by fitting it in a frame of wood made from a cigar box, using a piece of broken mirror to reflect light, he studied the microscopic world; the tiny animals and plants found in the fields and swamps.

At the age of six he constructed a rabbit hutch which was far superior to one built next door by a 30-year-old adult. It was about that time in his life that he performed a prodigious physical feat. This was the moving of a coal shed containing a half ton of coal for a distance of approximately 100 feet over soft ground and in between apple trees to a new and more convenient location. Using Archimedes' principle of the fulcrum and, with a half-dozen two-inch steel pipes, he raised the coal shed sufficiently high to use the pipe as rollers, sometimes moving the shed only a few feet a day; the whole project taking more than two weeks time.

At the age of eight, he won an argument with his father—who was, incidentally, a very learned man and a powerful orator—the subject of the argument being the nature of magnetic flux. Throughout his boyhood there were numerous examples of various accomplishments which would, to say the least, label him a prodigy; and no doubt, as can be reasonably supposed, separated him to a large extent from the usual normal associations which most boys have. He had little desire for sports such as various ball games, but weather permitting, he could be found about the fields and streams studying the innumerable and fascinating displays of biological life. And when the weather was foul, he would be reading books on psychology, medicine, philosophy, etcetera.

It is said that at the age of fourteen, one of his school teachers, a professor of biological sciences, placed a personal evaluation that he had an equivalent of a college education in many subjects at that time. However, his schooling was incomplete; hardly seventeen, his family migrated to California and he was forced to supplement his education by night classes and other extracurricular educational participation. As he has so aptly expressed it on a number of occasions, when asked about his education he said, "It was a close shave; I narrowly missed regimentation."

At this point it should be noted that only in a complete biography could full justice be given in describing what history may prove to be the most remarkable life lived in 2000 years. Indeed, it may well be that this person is, in the full scientific idiom of the twentieth century, reestablishing the Science of Life preached by Jesus, for there is a direct connotation in the life he lived at that time; and just as was Jesus, a member of the Essenic Brotherhood which formed that powerful but comparatively unknown background which made this mission possible.

At the age of twenty-three, the author entered into marriage; his strongest and most compelling reason was perhaps a desire to end the loneliness and apartness which he had felt all his life. He soon realized however, that his bride was mentally still a child; but from a sense of loyalty to the soon-to-be-born child, continued this marriage.

It was during this twelve-year period that he distinguished himself among his friends and people of his community with feats of outstanding clairvoyance. Using palmistry as sort of a stage prop, he would look into the past and prophesy the future to his friends and associates. Sometimes this was very disconcerting and, in several instances tragic predictions were made, accurately foretelling death. Then in 1941, just before World War II, this relationship with his wife was brought to a close as she left home stating that all the good that had ever come to her, her language, poise and general decorum, etc., she owed to his influence.

Freed from the ménage of household affiliations, he immediately entered into a phase of his life which can best be described as parapsychological in nature; going into the various churches and dance halls during the war years he would, during the course of the day and evening hours, give accurate descriptions, happenings, etc., of loved ones who were overseas in various theaters of war; and it was in this way, when regular communication was virtually impossible to those who waited at home, they were kept informed as to the whereabouts of their menfolk.

Then in 1947, he remarried even though he knew it was karmic and involved a great circumstance of the past, and which was absolutely necessary to work out in the present, removing an obstructing psychic block and helping establish his mission. He knew completely about this and on a number of occasions warned his bride-to-be the impending circumstances could be tragic in nature.

Then in 1950, at the exact date so prophesied, this event took place. A reincarnated priest, Caiaphus, who had lived in the Temple at the time of the crucifixion, (2000 years ago) and who was one of those responsible for this historical tragedy appeared on the scene. A very powerful and thoroughly evil person, openly and secretly practicing the arts of black magic, literally obsessed this wife; and through her and the love Ernest had for her, he (the former priest) descended upon him. Then for five days and nights a great battle was waged and, as Dr. Norman described it, "For five days and nights, I fought all the demons in hell."

At the end of that period, he emerged victorious but a marked man; for in the palms of his hands, he now carried the scars of his crucifixion 2000 years ago and in his mind, the clear and vivid memory of that lifetime which culminated in his crucifixion that eventful day on the hill of Calvary.

Then again, after being freed from this karmic marriage, he entered into another phase of his life and one which was marked by many unusual happenings and circumstances. During this period of time, many well-known clairvoyants and mediums, on different occasions described three white-bearded, white-robed, very old men who were accompanying him into their churches and carrying under their arms huge books with the inference that these were the books which, later on, would be brought into the world. These three men were later identified as Enoch, Ezra and Elisha.

Then in February of 1954, in an after-session, following a regular church conference meeting, these same three prophets were seen (psychically) and described by a visiting medium as standing beside Ruth—who "happened" to be attending that meeting. This, in itself, was prophetic and marked the beginning of a new era in both their lives. For, although up to that time strangers, in this present life, they were quickly brought together and married and, at that point, the true mission of Ernest Norman was entered into.

The first years spent together were chaotic ones, filled with innumerable and never-ending psychic experiences which to Ruth were not only amazing but often rendered her temporarily physically incapacitated so great was their intensity. And again, another biographical volume would be needed to best describe these years; how it was that Ruth took a shortcut, so to speak, into eternity, speeding up her evolutionary progress by thousands of years.

It was also at the beginning of this time that Dr. Norman entered into a new phase of his work—an extended psychosomatic science. Using his highly developed aptitude, he often looked back into the many past lives of his students, ferreting out and graphically describing the true originating causes of some vague present-day disease or disturbance. In this respect, his work gradually began to develop and unfold into an expanded Science of Life which gave the true causes and cures to all unknown and incurable diseases and which are now puzzling materia medica.

Even more important were the many miraculous healings which occurred when these causes were explained to those who suffered from some malignant or incurable condition. Nor was this work confined locally but, through the mails and using certain forms of advertising media, many people were contacted; some from remote countries, and invariably, when these persons began studying the now existing books and lessons they would begin to get well.

There is more, much more, which could be added to these brief depictions and which, in the future, will be more adequately served in a complete biography. The conclusion to this preface cannot at this time be finished nor will it be finished so long as mankind exists; for in the presentation of life, its various interdimensional elements and factors, as so posed by the author, will in the course of future history become a continuous, living testimonial to this man—a pioneer who has braved the persecutions and destructive reactions in order to pave the way for the future millennium when mankind will be more closely associated with and more expressionary, in life from the Inner or the Kingdom Within, as it has so adequately been described and demonstrated by this man.

NOTE:

This preface was compiled in the extreme necessity of acquainting any and all individuals who may be interested and, by reason of their interest, assumed to be in a receptive position whereby they can realize the great and tremendous importance of Unarius; and as the expressing element of Unarius, Ernest L. Norman and his life should therefore become known to those so interested. Inasmuch as his life was a constant succession of miraculous psychic demonstrations, these should be used as incontestable proof to those who may be wavering and need some bolstering power to crystallize their own efforts in faith.

Inasmuch as no written diary was kept, these various depictions were drawn from memory and dictated in the accustomed manner and delivery, as were all Unarius transcripts. In complete justification of the purpose involved and served, no attempt should be made to equate them in terms of personal relationships or which may be classified as an extruded ego. The author is quite aware of all psychological aspects involved and their impacts. So far as common denominators are used and in this frame of reference, all superlatives become inadequate to describe even one psychic experience; and this fact will be verified by anyone who has passed through the prescribed limits of mortal life and transcended into the realm of the psychic world. Therefore, the author feels fully justified in serving the common cause, which will inspire any individual to aspire to a higher way.

FOREWORD

In presenting to you this book, "The Voice of Venus", we do so with certain qualifications. Inasmuch as Unarius is an Interdimensional Science, and that it is primarily concerned with acquainting the student with the higher regenerative principles of life and, as this regenerative principle is pure science, the student must therefore rightfully assume that he must gradually break away from the various religious systems and their associated protocol and dogmas, replacing these more primitive and elemental concepts with the higher science of life.

It is therefore possible that the student may read in this and other Unarius books, certain phrases or words such as divine, prayer, pray, God, etc., which are part of these old primitive religious aspects but which are not a part of the Unarius teachings.

This book, "The Voice of Venus" being the first work in the series, "The Pulse of Creation", is therefore, by necessity, an inductive book which bridges the gap, so to speak, between the old materialistic world and the Higher Spiritual Worlds; and that such phraseology is so used by necessity rather than choice, as a way and means by which the student can gradually acclimate himself into a higher spiritual world which has no religions, no dogmas nor creeds; a world in which life is lived as an inductive oscillating principle with the Infinite, rather than from the baser, materialistic, reactionary way of the material world.

Therefore, dear student, if and when you come across such words or phraseology which seem to conflict with later and more purely scientific concepts of Unarius, do not challenge them in a critical way; nor should you be confused by them but rather, realize that these are merely comparisons, spoken in the idiom of the past; and like the past and all things connected with the past, must be left behind if you are to evolve into a higher world.

In that world God will cease to be some kind of an irascible, temperamental being, a segregationist, if you please, who marks the forehead of any human he so chooses with the stamp of his approval, supposedly giving him eternal life; and which is done on the basis of how well this person (or any person) so stamped has achieved merit by inflating the ego of his god either by sacrifice, proclamation, or any other means found to be suitable to appease this false god.

It must also be remembered that in these more immediate spiritual worlds which are described in the various books, such as Venus, Eros, Hermes, Mars, etc., many of the personalities were passing through the last stages of their material-spiritual metamorphoses; and that they still retain rather strong materialistic colorings which were reflected in some of the transmissions which largely comprise these books; and as they are individual dispensations, the author does not necessarily assume responsibility or verify such statements in the sense that they are inclusive factors in the Interdimensional Science of Unarius but realizes, just as the student should, that these renditions and their philosophies represent points of transition wherein an individual is passing from a lower to a higher plane of understanding.

One of the more ultimate achievements is in becoming, as has been mentioned, a conscious entity oscillating Infinitely and which, in the language of the earth man, could be called a god, with some differences in the concept of godhood, as portrayed by the earth man. He has always personified his god with his own attributes and propensities as well as the emotional side of human nature. It is the purpose of Unarius to destroy these false god ideologies and to replace them with a functional, re-creative, regenerative Infinite.

In any final analysis which may be entered into at any point in your evolution, the thought must always be kept uppermost in your mind: that whatever factors you have entered into in your analysis and, while these may represent the sum-total of your knowledge, never misconstrue these factors and such introspection as you have entered into as an absolute abstraction.

It is a common and most fallacious practice to condone or condemn various new aspects with the immediate particular perspective. New factors, new concepts, should represent to the individual a challenge which will test the strength and merit of his reasoning faculties.

It is the problem of each individual not to condemn or to try to destroy his future as it comes to him, but to try to understand it. In a normal evolutionary progression, the Infinite will always pose an infinite number of factors; some of these may be more acceptable on the basis that they may be comparative to the past, others may be totally unknown. Just as in animals, it is the nature of the elemental man to be fearful of the unknown and this fear gives him a reactionary and most destructive intent to destroy the unknown.

14

Therefore, a person can be truly said to be wise when all factors, known and unknown, can be mentally assimilated and digested as constructive elements and representative forms of consciousness which, when properly polarized with the infinite abstraction as posed by the Higher Self, eventually become a god-like entity. Unarius, therefore, should represent to you your millennium, a thousand or more years of living earth lives and lives in between earth lives, wherein you will pass through your material-spiritual metamorphoses. There will be many points of transition and many challenges and places where knowledge of principle, the power of reason and introspection will become your "savior". Should you fail to acquire this vital knowledge and fail to use it as the power behind your evolutionary progress, then you will fall.

This is the prime creative purpose of life which is a part and a way in which the Infinite lives and regenerates through every human.

THE VOICE OF VENUS

CHAPTER 1

Welcome to the Planet Venus

To the planet Venus, I bid you welcome for my people and for myself. I am known as an Avatar and I would show you some of our ways of life and some of the wonders of the spiritual realms. But first, in order to understand what might better be called a plane, or a dimension, as it is sometimes referred to by the people of the earth, we may liken these things to something similar to a large soap bubble which is being blown by a child with the familiar bubble pipe; and while the bubble is a thing of beauty and glows with iridescent colors, yet if we were to examine it under a powerful magnifying glass, we would find it even more wonderful; for here are microscopic particles of water, each one rounded and each one adheres to its neighbor by the law of adhesive relationship. And so, likewise is the great cosmic universe about us and the many suns and planetary systems, each one adhering to the others through the laws of great universal magnetic structures or lines of force; and countless suns make one star cluster which is known as a galaxy by your astronomers, and each galaxy is but a pinpoint of light in the great Celestial Universe.

Yet there are universes beyond universes, each one occupying a relationship something similar to the tiny water droplet in the soap bubble. And like the soap bubble which represents an adhesive mass of particles supported by other adhesive particles called the atmosphere, so likewise are the countless universes which are strung out through what you call space. They are likewise supported and maintain their relationship with what is called the material plane by other supporting structures which can be called, for want of a better name, dimensions. If we look at the beam of a searchlight we will see that from the point of emergence from the lens as it progresses further and further away from its source, it loses its brilliance and intensity. So likewise does your mind function.

If we visualize the energizing life force which is the sustaining and motivating factor in all things about you, such sustaining force must be of such frequencies or intensities that are compatible with your perception, for perception is necessary in all stages of soul evolution; and while the many dimensions or planes extend on and on into infinity, to your mind this infinity is somewhat likened to the searchlight beam and the further your mind must travel, more correctly to visualize such infinity. Such dimensions are not compatible with your present status of conception. These factors as they have been explained must be borne in mind before it is possible for the earth man to visualize such phenomena as flying saucers or space travel. Likewise it is extremely difficult for the earth scientist to conceive anything which is beyond his own realm or dimension and with such instrumentation as he has contrived to substantiate his limited perception.

It is one of the tasks of each individual in making his soul evolution that he must first set about to tear down his preconceived limited concepts. It has been said about many of the numerous scientists, as they call themselves on the earth plane, that they have contrived something of an understanding in their relationships with other dimensions such as the third, fourth, fifth, etc. Such a concept is like the child who picks up a handful of shiny pebbles and thinks that these are the only pebbles in the world. A dimension cannot be numbered, neither can it be called higher or lower than its neighbor, for a dimension is roughly an accumulation or spectrum of vibration which maintains a certain basic harmonic relationship.

It is one of the common fallacies of the earthman to believe that energy is destructive or that it is sinful. He must always remember that all energy has as its emanating source or fountainhead what is sometimes referred to as the Supreme Being in earth language; and while earth men may use or misuse energy in some destructive form yet it cannot remain destructive, for such is the way of energy from this Infinite Fountainhead. Thus through the evolution of time must it ever be and through the many lives of each individual, that while the individual is misusing energy destructively, he is unwittingly learning its proper usage. So the end result becomes one in which the Supreme Wisdom of the Fountainhead teaches all mankind, each in his own way, and therefore can never become destructive.

In our own planetary system the earth astronomer has found through his telescopes, various other heavenly orbs or bodies revolving in fixed orbits around our central sun and he has assumed from such external appearance or from studies made by refractory instruments that these planets, as he calls them, can or cannot sustain life as compared to the life about him on his own earth plane. Such a concept is extremely limited and baseless and while he calls himself a scientist he has not reached the point in his mental evolution where he can visualize anything beyond the spectra of his own 100 elements; and thus he has become like the child with the pebbles. Each and every planet in this solar system could quite possibly support life in one of the various innumerable dimensions which lie outside the realm of perception for the earthman.

It can also be said, that while the earthman sees about him many things which are completely intangible as far as his own perception is concerned, even though, ironically, he may have created these so-called intangibles, he may think he has the picture of the atom, yet he has never seen one. He may send pictures and sound through the air and yet he is not quite sure how this is done. Life for the earth scientist is an almost daily breakdown of many of the time-honored and treasured laws of the past. This has been going on for thousands of years, so likewise will the thousands of years of the future hold breakdowns of many of the ideas and laws which he has set up for himself at this day and time.

Through your mediumship you were given a factual picture of life on the planet Mars. This planet lies closer to your own spectra than any other of the planets of the solar system; in fact, one of your races of people is a migrant from this planet. Let it be said to the astronomers of your earth that they have not seen all of the planets of your solar system, for there are others which reside in different spectra and therefore cannot be viewed or analyzed by any means known to your earth people. The planet Venus has always been something of a great mystery to the earth astronomer because it seems to be shielded by what appears to be masses of clouds. This is erroneous. These so-called cloud masses or vapors are actually substances which reside outside of the realm or spectra of the 101 known earth elements. They are actually, in a sense, condensed masses of wave forms of high frequency energies which are kept like a protecting envelope around the planet through certain applied laws of frequency relationships.

This has been done purposely by the highly developed minds which live on Venus to avoid what would be an obvious state of confusion of the earth people inasmuch as, if they could see through their telescopes the actual surface of Venus and its radiant beauty as well as its completely different spectral analysis, it would not yield to any known scientific earth definition. The materials which compose this planet, while they might appear to be solid if you were standing there, are actually outside the realm of frequency relationships with which the earth people are familiar in their own spectra. In other words, it is something similar to your equation of water. While water is actually gas, in different temperatures it changes and becomes solid, liquid or gaseous. So likewise could any of your 100 known elements assume entirely different properties or relationships under different atomic frequencies and yet still remain the same reactive element.

Life on the planet Venus is in all phases and all relationships and does exist in an advanced state of harmonic frequency relationships. If an earth being was suddenly transported in the flesh to the planet Venus, he might find himself in a position similar to a man floating in midair in a steam room. While the same water vapor frozen on a surface could easily support him, it could not support him as steam or vapor. The earth scientist has to learn two basic facts about atomic structures. He has partially succeeded in this in molecular relationships, but has not visualized the same principle of conception in the frequency rate of vibration of the so-called atomic structures. Therefore the man with his earth-body on the planet Venus would more or less find himself in his earth-body and earth-mind in a world which was completely devoid of form and substance. Neither could he see any of that which was about him and he would quickly perish or separate himself from his earth-body in what is called death because of his lack of perception. Life on the planet Venus is made possible only to those who have evolved in their spiritual progression to a point where an entirely new and unlimited perception has become a vital and integrated working agent of their life force. Under such conditions, all phenomena such as is known to earth people, is a common part of the life of every Venusian.

Your own Avatar of Spiritual Science, whom you call Christ, demonstrated a factual working facet of this conception. In other words, the mind of each individual becomes an integrated working part of the great Fountainhead and, as such, an individual participant can and does direct this life-giving, all energizing, all constructive, all intelligent force into everything about him and into everything he does. For example, he does not need to do as the earth-man does in making his clothes—gather the wool or the blossom and go through the lengthy manipulative processes to construct these garments. Instead, the Venusian takes this vital, constructive, energizing force from the Fountainhead and so directs it through the science of his own mind, that it becomes the shining luminous garments about him. Likewise are his dwellings and all the things about him so constructed. But I see your earth-minds are tired and so I will leave you for the present but I shall return on the light frequency beam when conditions are proper and necessary. From the people of Venus I bid you Godspeed.

Your Brother,
Mal Var

CHAPTER 2

The Polarity Principle of Evolution

While speaking to you last time, I may have said some things which may have seemed very strange to you, for before taking an astral flight to Venus and witnessing a factual portrayal of what is to be seen there, it is necessary to go beyond the commonly accepted standards of earth life. Even the most learned men on your earth planet would be less than infants in our world. We do not wish to depreciate or to cause any man to feel a sense of inferiority because he has not progressed in his soul evolution to a point where he could visualize such things as are in this realm and dimension.

The thought patterns of mankind on the earth are such universally used and commonly practiced elemental thought patterns which have been relived basically throughout the pages of history. The thought pattern of the average earth person is very simple and elemental. He is taught and learns from infancy to compare all the things he sees about him in direct proportion to such outside or external stimulating agents as fear, pain or hate which induce certain reactive thought patterns within the child's mind. These are further strengthened and solidified with the passing of years and inasmuch as his fellowman about him is likewise so steeped in these traditional thought patterns, the net result is that he is continually at strife within himself and he takes recourse to factors of safety by some semblance of unified community or civic government which in all cases is only the determining factor of safety against other communities or nations.

All in all, such a reactionary thought pattern as is practiced individually and collectively among communities or nations becomes the agent of outward expression of the individual. The hatreds, fears, insecurities and other reactionary factors that form this conglomerate and collective mass of negation must and always does cause such calamities as wars, plagues and mass murders.

Contrast this reactionary way of life to one which has been described to you from your sister planet Mars or in somewhat a similar fashion, to those who evolve unto the planet Venus. While it cannot be said that a child here is born of the womb but rather, is a product of evolution from some spiritual plane of progression, yet the beginning of the life of an individual on the planet Venus can in many respects be likened to the periods of infancy, adolescence and adulthood. However, here the similarity ceases.

Usually such individuals arrive at our way of life with a conscious retained memory factor of all they have been before. There are none of the usually associated periods of loss of memory through some lower phase of reincarnation. So therefore the individual begins his life-cycle in something of a state of consciousness which you might call Mastership. The child, if he can be called such, is beginning his evolutionary cycle, though life on this planet is not concerned with the factor of self. He has long ago lost his personal sense of ego and its many fearful implications and assumed instead the cloak of state-hood which links him with the great and universal brotherhood which is not concerned with self but only with the betterment of the countless billions of his fellow-men who have not yet evolved into a state of spiritual maturity.

In direct contrast to the limited perspective which the earthman sees about him, the Venusian has before him the unlimited vistas of an infinite universe. Instead of being bound by fetters which are of steel-like strength and made of the substance of one's own fears and insecurities, he sees before him the limitless heights into which he may travel beyond the ends of time, as you measure it out to yourselves in your earth lives. In our previous discussion other factors were mentioned such as the relative values of what you call solid substance or mass and what is called energy. Many years ago, one of the more learned men of your earth attempted to explain the relationship of mass and energy. This man, working in conjunction with a college, attempted also to explain the transmission of energy. While these explanations, being more advanced than any previous explanations seem to satisfy the need of the present day generation and, while the earth scientists were advanced by their understanding and usage, yet one important and vital factor was missed.

This important factor, which should have been included in these hypotheses, was the element of frequency. Before I progress further, however, I must explain that the word frequency is used only for the want of a better word. In general terminology, as you understand frequency, it is the coming and going, or recurrence of successive movements which are related to time and space. A person may come and go into his home, the number of times being the frequency, or your electric house current is moved on the surface of the wire in short bursts or pulsations at the rate of 60 per second. Here again the elements of time and space are involved. In other dimensions, the term frequency would relate only to such movements of force or energy which have a basic fundamental relationship according to the circular path in which they travel. These things may be difficult for your earthminds to understand for many of the associated factors of your earth lives are interwoven with the elements of time and space.

Your next step of evolution may take many thousands of years to eliminate these elements from your thinking. Reasoning or logic, and the power of mental assimilation become comparatively easy in your new found freedom, for with the elimination of time and space you will be able to travel, as it were, mentally into other realms and dimensions, or recurrence of successive movements, and which meaning of frequency is just beginning to be basically understood by the earth scientist. He has found that with high pulsating currents through certain types of crystals, he can regenerate frequencies or vibrations up to a million times per second.

It makes little difference that he is still erroneously calling these frequencies sound, for sound in its true sense relates only to the spectra which can be conceived with the human mind. What the earthman has actually begun to find is a whole new world which he may call vibration, but which he will find from time to time will break down many of the strongly conceived so-called physical laws. One of the things the earthman must find out himself is that there are no laws. A law exists within his mind only as a preconceived principle and all the written laws in the world are not worth the paper they are written on simply because laws, whether civic or spiritual, resolve into the moral character of the individual.

Likewise, in approaching the great Fountainhead which we will call God, we will find that, contrary to belief, God has no laws. He has placed no restricting fetters upon your growth or your downfall. God in His infinite Wisdom knows that what is sometimes called sin, resolves only into preconceived notions of right and wrong which become pertinent vital issues with the spiritual evolution of the individual. But I am digressing. Getting back to the more, shall we say, elemental understanding of what is mass and energy, as I have pointed out, the frequency factor has not yet assumed its true relationship in the earth plane science. Man uses energy in many ways. This relates to the transmission of such energy in its many uses, in the world about him. He has not yet discovered, in a true scientific fashion, that the relationship of this frequency to atomic structures, as he calls them, is the basic underlying and determining factor in what he calls mass or weight.

Your Avatar Christ, who was at one time Master of Venus, explained this principle of relationship in a very simple way by walking upon water and by resurrecting himself from a stone tomb. In other words, by simply changing the basic relationship of the atomic structures within his body with the higher dimensions or the source, he became weightless and was able to pass through seemingly solid stone. While in such a condition of being weightless or without the appearance of solidity, the various atomic structures of His body, which you call elements, were not in the least changed in the relationship to your third dimension or earth structures, as you call them, except in factors of solidity and weight. In other words, they would have still been reactive in the chemical test tube or the spectroscope as such commonly designated elements which are known to compose your bodies. Likewise, all of the 101 odd elements which are known to earth scientists could be changed in their relationship to the higher dimensions or to the Fountainhead and would likewise become weightless and without solidity or, by the same token, be made so infinitely heavy that they would defy all your preconceived ideas of understanding.

Some of your earth astronomers have postulated a reasonable equation in their researches by declaring they have found a star which contains atomic structures so dense that a cubic inch weighs 2000 tons. May I again remind you that the terms weight, solidity, time and space are only factors which have been induced in your present-day earth life understanding. Therefore, a trip to Venus, if it could be assumed by any earth person in a physical body in which he walks about the earth, would find conditions on the planet Venus quite different than he may have anticipated. The astronomer on earth has succeeded to a certain degree in theorizing that certain chemical elements exist on or in the planet Venus which are similar to those on the earth; but lo, my friend, he would find to his surprise and chagrin that these elements are vastly different in his commonly accepted understanding of solidity or weight.

An ancient man of more advanced understanding, while sitting in his bath, found that each earth element such as silver and gold displaced, when immersed, different quantities of water. He was so elated by this discovery that he ran down the street naked, screaming, "Eureka, I have found it!" Even in your present day understanding, this so-called law of specific gravity has been displaced by a more accurate system of atomic weights. If the ancient man were living today in your world and time, he would not need to immerse the King's crown in water to find that the King had been defrauded and that it contained silver. I am pointing out this story to you that, in the course of history or evolution, man will and does, though sometimes ever so slowly, progress.

I could point out many and numerous displacements in physical laws which are related to the evolution of the earth people. Therefore, in the future, it can be justly prophesied that man will reach greater heights in his understanding of all the things about him. He will learn that his mind is bound only by his own preconceived notions. He will find, in breaking these bonds, the untrammeled, limitless, infinite vistas of God's Infinite Cosmos. He will also learn to lose the importance of his own selfish ego-consciousness and thus become what he must become; a vital, integral participant in a universal brotherhood of man.

CHAPTER 3

The Infinite Fountainhead of Light

Good evening. I am known as Sha-Tok. I will speak for Mal-Var as he will not be with you this evening. However, we all speak the same language so nothing will be lost. Mal-Var belongs to the council and is in the upper chamber this evening. In the two previous talks by my worthy brother, he discussed at some length a few of the underlying principles in the construction of what is called matter, and while these discussions seemed rather lengthy, it is necessary to prepare you; as otherwise, the true meaning of much that will be described to you or that you may see with your mind's eye may be lost.

In passing in review what has previously been explained, I hope that by now you will have begun to understand just what is meant by the relationship of mass and energy; and that mass and energy are all one and the same—the difference being in the way in which they are perceived according to such dimensional factors as time and space. In the atom, we find energy expressed in the relationship of time and space in such a way that it is seemingly solid or mass. The lightning which streaks through the sky or the light from the sun, is somewhat the same energy expressed in a different way with the factors of time and space.

Now that we have begun to understand the natural

phenomenon of energy, either as a moving dynamic force or as an apparently solid substance, we must not say that the expression or materialization of mass and energy is confined in what might be called the natural sequence of such manifestations as you are accustomed to in your daily lives. In other words, you will find individually in your soul evolution, your own particular cycle whereby you shall be able to use and direct energy from a higher dimensional plane through the channel of the mind and without the use of the hands. In your earth life existence, ideas are formed usually through the interrelative thought processes. In order to materialize such an idea, it must be worked out with the various materialistic processes which you have evolved in your daily transmission of life.

The use of familiar everyday objects about you were all originally such ideas. The watch which you wear on your wrist or the machine you call the automobile are all products of countless ideas and were brought into materialization only through a great deal of work and experimentation. In a more highly evolved state of consciousness such an idea of materialization would of course seem very crude. Such negative qualities as fear, human error, tolerances and production failures do not enter in. Such a highly evolved mind conceives, visualizes and realizes the infinite perfection of universal energy which stems from the Fountainhead.

Such energy needs only the proper directive channel to individualize its potentialities. You people of the earth have often called this energy God; and as has been explained, as God, it is Infinite, so He must express not only infinity but infinite individualism. It is that Infinite Wisdom of God which has conceived that by the creation of man He has individualized Himself and, that as man exists in the countless planes and dimensions in which God expresses and lives in the Infinite, so He also likewise expresses Himself in all these realms and dimensions in a finite way.

Therefore, my friends, we must not say that I am better than such a man or look down on someone whose skin is of a different color. Likewise must we love everybody, for if we love not them, how can we love our God who has created Himself in a finite way in every man? Now that we have discussed our relationship with the Infinite Creator, we can begin to visualize that it is indeed a great and sacred thing and one of holy trust when in this stage of evolution we find ourselves an open, directive channel for this God-force. And yet here again is God expressing infinity; for in all other roles He has assumed the supreme position of the Master Creator. So now he becomes in a finite way subservient through the channel of man's mind. This has been expressed in a lesser degree in the creative ideology of the people of the earth and of similar planes; God, there, as in all other places, still being the prompting, uplifting Overlord, in assuming the role of Mastership, God and his wondrous Creative Power and Wisdom, became the complete obedient servant of the individual; for now the individual can direct this Creative Intelligent Energy in such a manner that it will create all of the things that the individual deems necessary for the time and place.

The Avatar Christ, in performing his miracles, did just this. The stories of the various healings are those in which the creative life energy of God was so directed that it became healed flesh. A closer analysis of this process would reveal that this creative structure was followed by a secondary instantaneous regrouping into molecular structures that thus became healed. You may ask how it is possible for the mind of an individual to assume Mastership over God—as it may at first appear. This is not correct. We must remember that the individual is God, only in a finite, personalized form and, in expressing individualized personality, has assumed a correct and delicately balanced relationship with infinite God.

On the planet Venus, we all who are living here, have taken our first step in the relationship of such Mastership. It is here in our daily lives that we put into practice this harmonious, creative relationship with the Fountainhead in all of the acts of our daily lives. Mind is the creative principle using and directing this God force in the creation of all the essentials of life.

As was touched upon previously, your familiar sense of mass or solidity would be valueless here. All atomic structures which compose this planet and all of the things about it do not, shall we say, vibrate in the same plane of relationship from the emanating source of the Fountainhead. Therefore, your five physical senses, of touch, taste, smell, seeing and hearing would be quite useless here as they have been evolved to function in atomic structures and frequencies which were of a lower and different relationship to the Fountainhead. However, to us our world is, in a general sense, quite as solid as yours.

Our various functions of sight, sound, hearing, smell and feeling are of course evolved to function in this particular plane or dimension. Here again I must draw a similarity picture. While you say in a spiritual sense God supplies your every need, yet you find it necessary to plant the seed and harvest the crop; or you must mine and smelt metal—or in whatever particular direction you may look, you must engage in work for the necessities of life.

33

In our world God is likewise the Fountainhead of all supply, however, we do not find it necessary to earn the daily essentials with the sweat of our brow. In our understanding God has become the supreme energizing force which feeds our bodies, which clothes us and which in short, does everything for us without the expenditure of time and energy or a great preponderance of machinery. I may point out that in your Bible you will find accounts of certain Avatars or Holy Men who fed themselves directly from the Fountainhead and so lived for many days without food or drink passing their lips, nor did they suffer any discomfort in so doing.

Tonight we are ringing a great golden bell in the central chapel so that its vibrations will carry across the distances which separate us in a physical sense from mankind who lives on many planets and each note of this golden bell carries with it the united and concerted prayer of love and goodwill to man wherever he may be found.

On the next occasion my brother Mal-Var will attend you. Until then I, Sha-Tok, wish upon you all the graces of the Almighty God.

CHAPTER 4

The Science of Space Travel

Greetings again, my friends, and all my brothers and sisters on the earth plane. May I say first that I am very happy to be with you again and to thank you for the gracious way in which you received my brother during my enforced absence. I have decided that inasmuch as you have begun to understand that the factors of energy and mass are but relative and that they depend primarily for expression upon the source or Fountainhead and that these equations of energy and mass are but the outward intelligence expressed from the Fountainhead. I have been very anxious that you understand this principle thoroughly. And it is partly because of this that I will discuss the topic of today which, although it does not necessarily pertain to the expression of life on Venus, is pertinent and vital for your understanding and peace of mind in the future generations of mankind upon the earth plane. Our topic today will deal with spacecraft and the historical background of the earth with regard to interplanetary travel.

When your scientists touched off the first atom bomb, it had an immediate and far-reaching effect into many of the astral worlds and in some of the dimensions which are more closely related to the earth. About five planets including Venus were immediately startled and gravely concerned with what might be the misuse of atomic power. Clarion, another planet not generally known to the earth people, was another one so concerned; likewise Mars. Eros also was alerted and was swung into an orbit which would bring it in close conjunction with the earth. These planets all sent out spacecraft or used other means to explore the earth to find out all possible ramifications which might be involved in these atomic explosions.

The people of the earth, during the following years, were tremendously excited by the appearance and strange behavior of these various types of craft. One type in particular which you call flying saucers has caused the greatest consternation and conjecture, particularly to the earth scientist. He is at a loss to explain the sudden appearance and disappearance of these craft. Also he is flabbergasted with the tremendous speeds which they can attain and which he can only track on his radar screen. He is also bewildered by their appearance of being at a white-hot heat or cooling to a dull cherry red. To interject a little mystery here, let me say there is no heat produced in the use of these craft. But first I must digress to explain to you some of the historical background which is necessary to understand your present situation.

About 500,000 years ago, the people of Mars were commuting regularly to the earth by spacecraft. They had established a colony on the southern edge of what is now called the Gobi desert at the foothills of the Himalayan mountains. They were however set upon from time to time by savage bands of native earthmen who roamed about the earth at that time. In the last of these forays, a large group of Martians barely escaped with their lives into the nearby hills where they remained hidden and lost to their countrymen who finally abandoned the idea of colonization on the earth. They were a peace loving people and although they had weapons at their disposal that would have annihilated these savage earthmen, yet they refused to use them; and so the earth swung in its orbit, unattended for several hundred thousand years until the coming of the Lemurians from the planet Lemuria which is about 700 light years (figured in our planetary system of light measurement) away from our solar system. You may wonder how these men traversed this vast distance without consuming the best part of their lives. It was through the principle of change of frequency relationship which enabled the spacecraft to travel through inner space at speeds approximately ten times that of your known speed of light (186,000 miles per second). Therefore the distance from Lemuria to our solar system could be traversed in a very small fraction of the time which you might assume would normally be necessary; in other words, about 5 or 6 years. During this journey the ship was flown and controlled by a robot calculator. The eleven who occupied the ship remained in a state of suspended animation, something like a cataleptic hypnotic trance.

It was about 160,000 years ago in your earth time that the great spacecraft crashed on the Gobi desert very close to where the Martians formerly lived. Inside were these eleven men on this craft which had come, as you have been told, from a planet much closer to the central vortex of the material universe and our own solar system. This was the planet Lemuria, about three times the size of the earth and warmed by the rays of a huge, brilliant, copper-colored sun to which it was fairly close. The people of this planet are, compared to your earth people, of a very large and tall stature. They are also advanced in their spiritual evolution to a point which is about one-half way between the scientific plane of Mars and the spiritual plane of Venus.

We had long been in telepathic communication with these people and it had been their first attempt with spacecraft at such vast distances which had ended so disastrously on earth. It had not been their desire to land on earth but rather on Venus, but they had been deflected from their true course by the strong magnetic field of a huge sun they passed on their journey here.

You are all somewhat familiar with the story of Mu or Lemuria on your earth; and how the science of these eleven Masters or Supermen was handed down through the ages so that it became a vital science of that civilization you call Atlantea. It was the people of Atlantea who still used spacecraft and were, through the knowledge and use of the principle I have explained to you, able to float silently through the air in weightless craft which they propelled by using force beams or energy beams, using as their source of energy the magnetic fluxes which surround the earth.

Near the close of this civilization there was a great deal of corruption which began to enter into a heretofore very wonderful way of life and which was something like the Utopia which the philosophers are wont to talk about. It was at this time that an Avatar who was living on Venus, made a pilgrimage to Atlantea and there, after proving his Mastership by placing the flame of life upon a crystal-clear quartz block which he materialized from energy, he ruled for the space of 428 days, during which time he wrote a book about life and placed it beneath the flame. It was his warning when he left that nothing should be taken from or added to this book or else Atlantea would perish. Your history will tell you the sad tale. Sometime after the disappearance of the Avatar, whom you call Christ, a group of Atlantean men, women and children, wishing to preserve their way of life, escaped in a spacecraft to Mars. It was the descendents of these people who were contacted by your earthman named Fry*, as well as numerous others. I am bringing you this story so that I can show you how these craft or flying saucers work and which will also point out to your earth scientists the underlying principles which they are now hopelessly trying to duplicate. The trip the earthman took in this flying saucer was quite real; however, it did not take place in the dimension or realm with which he is familiar.

This saucer is guided by a mother ship which is a cigar-shaped craft which usually hovers motionless out in space at about 10,000 miles distance from the surface. The craft is pilotless and is flown by a beam of energy which projects like an invisible searchlight from the mother ship. This beam is hollow like a tube, in the center of which the saucer always remains. The outer shell of this tube-like beam is a composite form of innumerable wave shapes or intelligences, which have been taken from a source coming from the Fountainhead and through processes which are known to them as well as to ourselves, these energies are so directed that they can change the relationship of the atomic structures which compose the metals of the ship and thus render it weightless, as it does not now in this condition, reside in the spectra of atomic frequencies which are subject to the gravitational pull of the planet earth.

This gravitational field, by the way, is merely a highly charged field of force which has as its origin a condition caused by friction between the outer shell of the earth and the inner **molten core. Now as I have told you, contrary to general belief, there is no heat involved in the glowing appearance of a flying saucer. This is caused simply by reflection and re- fraction similar to that principle which causes a rainbow. In other words, as the basic frequency rela- tionships of the atoms composing the metals are changed these atoms will, in assuming their place in molecular structures, reproduce such reflection or refraction from various light sources, such as sun- light, daylight or moonlight. The sudden stopping and starting of these strange craft is now likewise more easily understood.

If you have watched the pencil-like beam of a searchlight piercing the sky at night, you will see its extreme tip move at a tremendous rate of speed across the sky and yet, if you are standing by the searchlight, you would see that it moves very slowly and but a few inches at a time. This is exactly how these saucers are operated. They are flown up and down, over and around and in any direction the operator chooses by simply moving the searchlight beam projector. As I have explained, this beam is a hollow tube of energy and by the simple law of ad- hesive energy the saucer could not get out of this beam.

Now I see that your bodies are beginning to tire, although I know your minds are eager for more infor- mation. On my next visit I will give information which is more pertinent to life on Venus. I have brought you the topic of discussion today for several obvious reasons. Inasmuch as all of the underlying principles, as well as the motivating factors are all interwoven, they are of concern to all races or groups of people who are in a more advanced state of evolution than the earth peoples. I might add one thing more before I leave as I have heard you question the validity of flying saucer contacts or of other such similar ap- pearances of spacecraft to seemingly obscure people.

These are primarily somewhat in the nature of testings or psychological experiments and have been meant in a mild way to shock the earth-people from their ruts of materialistic complacency. You are right about one thing however. We, or any other advanced race, do not and would not seriously affect your own chosen way of life. It is the Infinite Wisdom of the God who created you in your finite way, that you must find your way back to the Fountainhead by developing your own spiritual evolution. And so until such future time I will await your convenience.

Brother — Mal Var.

*   Daniel W. Fry, author of "The White Sands Incident".
** Molten core being the term used by the earth scientists for the innermost center.

CHAPTER 5

Piercing the Cloud Cover of Venus

Judging by the thoughts which are received by me from you, you are quite anxious that we shall begin our exploration directly on the planet Venus. This I will be most happy to do, as I believe that by now your minds have been sufficiently freed from the bondage of the limited earth-life concepts around you.

I do not wish to be misconstrued in my attitude regarding your earth planet. It is a wondrously conceived and properly constituted place of life for people in your particular phase of development; and while your history reveals that there have been some good cycles and some not so good, yet with all it can be said that you are admirably situated in a world which was conceived as a battleground and testing place between your emotions and carnal desires and as an actual starting place in your spiritual evolution.

Of course I am making an exception of the many great old souls who have reincarnated from time to time into your way of life; and by the substance and strength of their wisdom have acted as a leavening agent which was a vital and necessary factor in maintaining the continuity of life in the lower orders of development in which they were working. Perhaps at some later time I will give you some more pertinent facts which will relate to the future history of your planet for not only is your past history well-known to us here on Venus, but your future has also been written.

In going to the planet Venus I will ask one thing of you; that you must remember that while you may see some things which may in some way remind you of your more familiar planet, yet as I have explained, there is nothing similar or comparable to what you call weight or mass. All things on Venus do have weight and solidity but only to those who have evolved into this plane and are properly constituted so that the elemental substructure of their minds and bodies is in close relationship with the elements around them, which is, of course, exactly the same relationship which your minds and bodies bear toward the elemental structures of the earth plane, the difference being, if you will pardon my being repetitious, in the relationship of that hackneyed word "dimension". I do not like this word as it has a confining sound and relates to such limitations as measurements or is suggestive of limited, confined spaces. However, I must speak in your language and in such a way as you will best understand me.

Now that we are on common ground we shall approach the Planet Venus and begin what I hope will be a profitable as well as enlightening venture, as has been done many times before. We will use as our vehicle our astral body and with our mind firmly ensconced within its comforting closeness, we will see what happens. But lo, I have hardly spoken before we are there, at least to our first stopping point, which is somewhat outside the astral shell of the planet; or as your astronomers call a similar one around the earth, the ionosphere. This astral shell around Venus differs somewhat from that of the earth planet. However, such differences are not so important as to warrant a further discussion. We will instead, merely say that its function is somewhat similar to that of the earth and that it is a protective shield against some of the dangerous radiations which come from various sources in outer space. Your astronomers, in looking at this planet, see only vague masses of cloud-like substances which seem at all times to be a complete envelope. Actually no earthman has seen the surface of the planet through a telescope or with any other device he may use in conjunction with these optical instruments.

I would like to point out that there are many earth people who have visited the planet on astral flights and have returned to earth with different and varying versions of their experiences. This is very easily explained as they see everything in direct proportion to their particular stage of spiritual evolution. Many people could take a trip around the earth and while they may all see the same sights, no two people can describe these things in the same way nor do they see them in the same way. This factor is much more manifest in their astral flights to Venus and in seeing what they do, inasmuch as the factors relating to conception are of a much more spiritual nature. Their thought patterns and philosophies in their earth life have preconditioned them so that they mentally select, as it were, such facets of perception as are compatible to these thought patterns.

However, I believe that through the channel of your mind, we here on the planet Venus, can express and describe to the earth people a somewhat broader and more scientifically factual concept of what we actually have here. There are, unfortunately, very few clear channels and even much that has been given has been wasted on the desert sands of the minds of the average earthman. It was hinted previously regarding the appearance of Venus that as it appeared to be cloaked in cloudy masses, the earth astronomers naturally drew the conclusion that Venus was a wet or watery place and that any life on this planet would therefore have to be aqueous in nature. This is only partially true. While there are clouds in the atmosphere of Venus, they are not wet, damp, vaporous masses but the moisture which is needed to support the luxuriant growth of vegetation. I can assure you that the planet is anything but aqueous.

In explaining the vaporous cloud mass appearance let us refer back to our original concept and that is —the relationship of elemental substances. They are due to the difference in relationship of atomic structures which compose the planet's atmosphere and the difference of frequency vibration rates.

This, of course, therefore makes these structures invisible to the earthman in what he conceives to be around the planet. He has simply jumped to the wrong conclusion that because he may see this envelope as a cloudy mass, that he may be able to obtain some refractory analysis. This may lead him further astray in his diagnosis for he has seen nothing more than that which is contained in our extra heavy thick ionosphere and the very deep atmospheric envelope which, of course, surrounds the entire planet.

Venus has no axis inclination as has your earth, therefore there are no seasonal changes. It is roughly one-third larger than the earth and is also much closer to the sun. I will not give you the figures on our Venusian measurements as we have small use for such things, but if you wish to satisfy your curiosity, any of your encyclopedias will give you this information. We here on Venus have an entirely different concept of time and space and such concepts as are used by the earth astronomers are somewhat reminiscent of the days when we, as children on a similar planet, played with mud pies. Getting down further into the atmosphere of our planet, we will begin to see many strange and (at least to your eyes) wonderful sights. The surface of this planet encompasses many and highly diversified geological formations. There are many vast mountain ranges, great lakes, rivers and oceans. You may think at first that this reminds you of your own planet, yet there are many differences.

The air itself does not seem to be as heavy but it gives you a wonderful feeling of exhilaration. This is due partly to the fact that Venus has a much more highly charged magnetic field. This, in combination with other factors, creates a gas somewhat similar to ozone which you may remember having smelled after a thunderstorm. There are other differences which relate to weather conditions and the lack of your more familiar seasonal changes, due to the difference in the intensity of the magnetic structure of the atmosphere and the ionosphere.

All such weather factors are much less violent than on your earth. Also we must remember that all elemental structures surrounding this planet are much closer in their linkage or relationship to the Fountainhead; and, shall we say, more intelligent and less obstreperous. There are none of the cold winters or snowy regions on this planet. Neither are there the vast arid desert regions or the steaming hot jungles. All in all, the planet is a much more well behaved vessel of life; partially, as I have said, because of a more highly evolved structural density and partially because we here on this planet know how to control weather conditions.

The Avatar Christ calmed the raging seas and caused the winds to cease their howling and then boldly walked upon the face of the now calm water. May I say humbly that we here on Venus also know of these things. Another thing which you will notice is the iridescent, glowing beauty; also the vegetation itself may display a riotous beauty of color and contrast, the seas and waters have a radiant opalescent beauty, and the very mountains seem to be composed of the essence of mother-of-pearl. All over, and about and around all of this, there are hanging multitudes of rainbow-hued auras. Dewdrops shoot forth radiant shafts of light which are far more brilliant than any you have ever before witnessed.

You may see a countless number of strange and fantastically hued birds and huge butterflies whose wings seem to be incrusted with a million jewels. You may taste the waters of some tumbling stream and find them sweet beyond all previous taste experiences. Or you may come upon one of the many cities which seem to hang half-suspended between earth and sky, which may remind you somewhat of the pictures in some childhood fairy book of the fairy castle on top of a high hill. Yes, my friends, Venus is a wonderful, beautiful place and a rich reward which may be well earned through the many thousands of reincarnations and earth lives.

On my next visit we will seek out one of these fairy castle-like cities and we shall enter in and meet some of those who have earned and richly deserve this reward; and yet even as it must always be so, our respective planes of life are so widely separated that we must return to our respective positions, but we will meet again soon.

Brother—Mal Var.

CHAPTER 6

The Non-Atomic Nature of Life

Although only a few hours have passed since my last visit, conditions are so propitious that it was deemed advantageous that I again make contact. I hope that you will pardon my intrusion in your daily earth life routine.

So we will resume our little trip where it was left off the previous evening. Now we are again back on the surface of Venus and we find ourselves standing in a beautiful forest glade and although it is quite familiar to me, I see in your mind that you are almost overwhelmed with the beauty. For the benefit of your earth brothers, let us sit down upon this grassy bank beside a pool so that I may not only explain more fully these things about you, but that I may also clear up some of the salient points which I see are not quite transparent.

As you look about you, you see many tall trees which stretch hundreds of feet into the air, and the overhanging branches seem to reach out and form a canopy which delicately laces the radiant solar energy that comes from the great golden orb which shines above; and while it is the same sun which shines on your earth it has here quite a different appearance, not so small and white or extremely brilliant, but it is large and of a soft golden yellow color which can be easily looked into.

As you have been told, the sun is not as commonly supposed, a mass of disintegrating atomic energy which is dissipating itself at white hot heat, but is instead a radiant energy projector which converts energy and reflects its light and other associated energy fluxes into what you term your three dimensional world. This energy source is, of course, the Fountainhead.

Due to the difference in atomic constituents and frequency vibration in the atmosphere and astral shell of Venus, the sun is therefore able to transmit or reflect a somewhat different frequency spectra upon Venus' lower orders of the more actinic rays being properly filtered out, as these rays are merely byproducts in frequency transmission from the radiant source or sun.

I see that you are looking about you and gazing with wonder and awe at the display of the many strange and different species of plant, bird and insect life.

Over there is an orchid-like plant which thrives on air and which has a blossom so large you could easily lie down in it. Floating upon the surface of the lake, you see another aqueous plant growing before you, exactly similar to the one you call the lotus which was brought to your earth by one of your Holy Men who had made an astral flight to this planet and had actually lived here at one time. However, it is impossible at this time to describe all of these many and wonderful flowers and trees and the busy insect and bird life which lives and flourishes among them. Let it be said however, and you'll agree with me on looking about you, that it exceeds beyond the wildest reach of the imagination, what an earthman might be capable of envisioning.

Many earth people have, in moments of psychic

49

transmission or experience, caught a glimpse of this fairyland you see about you and thought they were in Heaven and while this is partially true in comparison to your earth planet, yet we here on Venus are still in a comparatively low state of evolution and we are now able to see that stretching far ahead of us there are various and innumerable realms or planes which far exceed our Venusian planet not only in beauty but in a spiritual way of life in which the people of those places live.

As I have told you previously, some of the more spiritually advanced peoples of the earth have had contacts or flights to Venus, several of whom are living in your day and age. However, they have all returned with different and diverse reports as to what they have seen on this planet. As I have said, this is of course due to the extent of their spiritual perception. You may liken the planet Venus in certain ways to your earth world. As you know there are countless expressions and ways of life upon your planet. There are the savages in the jungle, as you call them, and there are the Orientals; there are numerous separations which you call nations, each maintaining a distinct and separate way of life which is characterized by differences of clothing, speech, forms of government and so on.

In all your previous accounts of the planet Venus you may have been given the impression that there was only one race or type of people living here. This is entirely erroneous. There are many kinds of people living on this planet, the difference being, however, in the stage of their spiritual evolution or position in the spectra of frequency vibration into which they have automatically gravitated. It is somewhat like the keys upon the piano which are divided into groups and octaves. Your earthman divides these frequency vibrations into relative planes of consciousness as physical appurtenances. It is different on Venus, inasmuch as the physical does not exist in your generally conceived idea of material or physical. Therefore, such divisions as planes or strata reside in a spiritual concept.

When a discarnate entity evolves through time unto the planet Venus, he usually finds himself in one of the lower states of consciousness. He will therefore, through time (as you call time) or cycles, incarnate or evolve to this planet and if he is advancing properly he will each time re-materialize into a higher state of consciousness.

On your earth planet the divisions of life are very strongly marked in the physical or material sense. The black man born and raised in the jungle would not feel at home living among your modern skyscrapers. Therefore, there are mental as well as geographical separations. On Venus this is somewhat different. We might liken them to the differences or levels in one of your skyscrapers; and while all of the people here remain in harmonious relationship with each other as they are vitally interested in each other's welfare, they of course know, as individuals, their proper place in the scale of their evolution on this planet.

Because you have not yet been completely separated from your physical body and have therefore not advanced in your perceptions, you will have to remain content and satisfied with seeing the dimension or plane upon which I, in my plane and those who are like me, are living. So to avoid confusion, you will not be permitted to see the lower realms of consciousness which exist on this planet.

Let it be said, however, that the terminology of lower and higher is used only because your vocabulary is so limited and does not include the proper phrase-ology which would clarify the meaning. Even the very lowest form of man upon our planet could be considered as similar to an Adept or Guru, as you call them on your planet. He has already begun to learn to break away from the more bestial way of life such as is found on the lower earth planes.

You people of the earth spend all but a very few hours of each day in catering to the needs of your body. You must feed it, sleep it, bathe it and other-wise pamper it and yet you must otherwise use it or misuse it in gaining more and more of the things to pamper it with. You have become so steeped in the fears which are induced by pain and insecurities, that you have incarcerated numbers of your kind because they have become so weak in mental and physical ways that they have broken down in your treadmill-like existence; and while so incarcerated, they are treated even more like animals and guards with whips and guns are placed over them and they are chained or beaten, or perhaps shocked into insensibility.

Such things are indeed crude and barbaric and do not belong in the consciousness of a man who supports such a system six days a week and supposedly worships his God on the seventh. And so to further increase this great travesty against his God he must arm his children with the destructive weapons of aggression and send them out to kill his neighbor's children.

Yes, my friend, even the beasts of the field which you use for food are not so unintelligent. But let us get back to my people. As I have said, we possess no physical bodies in your sense of the physical; neither are we born on this planet, as you would call birth by your standards. When a person from another spiritual plane wishes, for reasons of his own evolution, to live on this planet, he first seeks out in a spiritual way, a plane or place in which he feels most harmonious and which will be most conducive to his proper growth. He will then seek out a family and a community and make his presence and his wishes known. They in turn will, through the power of their minds, project energy and build for him a body in which he can enter and thrive upon this planet.

This is somewhat like your materialization seance but in a much more advanced and practical form, inasmuch as the participants themselves, or as you call them, the mediums, actually become the parents of the newborn, materialized being. Sometimes however, the newly entered entity is not accustomed to supporting his body in its new environment and it must therefore be from time to time refreshed and rebuilt by his parents. Sooner or later however, the newly born individual grasps the idea by using the radiant energy and through his mind will project it into this body and thus keep it alive and vigorous.

On your earth planet you must eat foods, which are transformed into energy by a reflex digestive system so that your bodies may survive. On Venus, however, there is no eating in your commonly accepted concept. Our digestion is processed through the mind into our bodies and becomes an automatic process, which of course leaves us much more time for the better things of life.

Just in case you may think this a bit preposterous, remember that energy is energy in whatever form it may assume. Your earth scientist has already harnessed the solar energies in countless ways for your comfort and convenience. Even the battery in your automobile has stored energy which was originally sunlight in a bygone age, which came down to you stored up in carboniferous deposits or petroleum and has been converted back to energy through the process of combustion which turns the generator, thus reactivating the battery.

As you can easily see by now, we have engaged in what is quite likely to turn out to be a very detailed and lengthy dissertation upon our planetary way of life and that it is quite different than your way. You must therefore take it in small doses, if I can so use this term, as I know the limitations of your earth minds; and as I would avoid any confusion, therefore let us rest for a while and I will return after a suitable interval. So until then, this is Mal-Var, can I say, "Signing off"?

CHAPTER 7

Azure Crystalline City of Splendor

The goodness of the evening to you, brother, and as you seem a little surprised to find yourself back sitting beside the lake where we left off this morning, may I say that I took the liberty to set you back in this same spot after receiving the impulses from your mind.

I believe we were discussing matters pertaining to the emergence, or shall I use the word birth, into our planetary way of life. There are also other aspects which relate to the absorption of radiant energies into our bodies which replace your familiar intestinal tract. Of course by now you will have begun to cast about you and have found many heretofore seemingly unnoticed examples which are in every sense just as miraculous. Each tiny leaf and blade of grass carries on this radiant energy process. Your own bodies, using the lower orders of intestinal absorption, could not do so without the direct interpolation of this intelligent radiant energy; and while all of these things have been almost unnoticed, nonetheless, each and everything about you and within you carries its own message of its conception from the Infinite Fountainhead.

But come, let us walk toward the mountain which you see in the distance; and do not be surprised if your walking has lost the laborious physical effort or that you seem to float. As you are somewhat used to astral flights, however, I do not feel you will find any great difficulty in adjusting yourself.

While we are progressing toward the city, may I say that you will quite likely see things which may stretch to the utmost your powers of conception. All things on Venus, including the substructures which compose the planet itself as I have said, in their own spectra, have a relationship to the Source or Fountainhead which is much closer, or shall I say in a higher stage of evolution. Therefore, those elemental substances, as you will see, will reflect in consequence an outward expression which has a great deal more perfection and beauty. On your earth you have similar examples of this evolution. The soft black carbon in a higher state becomes the sparkling diamond. Likewise, many of the darkened masses of metal may enter, in an oxide form, into some other siliceous material and give to it the radiant hue of the ruby or the blue cool depths of the aquamarine. In fact, your gems are direct transmutations of these lower orders of elemental substances into a higher frequency expression.

The earth chemist has, in this last age, learned to tremendously alter things by the rearrangement of molecular structures, and while he must use tremendous quantities of caloric energy, he will no doubt someday find a much easier and less costly way to not only change molecular structures, but he may actually find a way to alter the frequency relationship of the substructures themselves.

But see, now we are approaching one of our fairest and largest cities and as I said previously, it does seem to hang suspended between earth and sky but you will soon discover that it is actually resting on the top of a huge mountainous mass of what might be called perfect crystal. In your normal relationship, that is, if you are actually living on this planet you would see that this crystal mountain was actually reflecting all of the colors of the rainbow from the many facets or prisms which go to make up this huge mass. However, as you are not properly attuned to all of the spectra or light radiant sources, you will see this simply as a mountain of clear transparent sparkling crystal. But come, here is the pathway. Yes, I see you are wondering how such a small pathway could serve such a large city and, as you have correctly surmised, there are many thousands of people living in what looks to you like some creation which you may have seen painted for you and shown in one of the darkened halls you call movie theaters.

Transportation in these higher Venusian realms is not, as you might suppose, a problem which is solved by the use of various types of vehicles. We have no need for them, as we all travel freely about in the inner plane of consciousness; in other words, in something in a more highly evolved state than what you call astral flight. Your Holy Men, including the Avatar Christ as well as many hundreds of adepts, traveled about the earth in the same manner. This is, however, almost a forgotten science among your earth people of today and only some of your seekers of truth know the history of past ages in which this form of travel was commonly used by these advanced souls.

Now that we have reached what appears to be the main thoroughfare of our city, you will notice that it is built upon a flat plain, which is the actual top of this crystal mountain. For convenience, if you wish, we will call this city Azure. There are, of course, many other cities which are built upon much similar masses of more highly evolved atomic structures which can be called mountains. In the lower orders of evolu-

The Crystal City of Azure

tion, the people of this planet have built their cities upon the flat plains or valleys in more suitable places which have relationship to streams of water, which some of these people still seem to think is necessary for the existence of such cities. If you are a bit puzzled by this, it is because some of these lower orders of evolution which have evolved onto this planet, still carry with them the strong remembrances and associations of lower earth lives in which eating, and drinking, and other things which they used to do, have not been entirely eliminated through the lapse of sufficient numbers of incarnations.

Venus is, roughly speaking, a place where a person loses the last vestiges and remnants of those earth life thought patterns; and, as I have said, he will evolve through many reincarnations to and from this planet until he emerges a full-fledged spiritual being. When I speak of earth lives, I am not necessarily referring to your earth, as there are countless numbers of such planets, not only in this Universe but in the countless Universes throughout what your astronomer calls space. All of these planets, of course, have their sister planets which have a higher place in their order of evolution, just as in the case of your earth and Venus. However, I see that you are somewhat perplexed as you look about you, for you are wondering how you may best describe all of these things which you see about you.

One thing more, however; I have purposely made it impossible for you to see my people until a little later on. This will avoid confusion and complication. They will also not be able to see you, nor will you suffer any embarrassment in case you accidentally meet someone, as you will pass right through them or they may pass through you. This can be done, of course, because you are in a different frequency vibration. A little later on when your curiosity is somewhat satisfied, we will change this situation so that you will be able to see and talk to some of my brothers and sisters.

However, as I said before, I am using the utmost caution and discretion for I do not wish to disturb or shock the earth minds who may read your words. Not that we are not pleasing as to appearance; I believe you will find us so and not too much different from the reflection you see in your own mirror, except that you may be able to see much more clearly the auric colors which surround our bodies. As we are in a higher frequency rate we are therefore, can I say, much more dynamic; so much more so, that we may appear to radiate light.

However, let us enter one of the larger homes here which is standing close by. As you will see, they are all of tremendous size; and even though we are on an average but slightly taller than the earthman, yet we would find that the small cubicles which he calls homes would be to us extremely cramped and confined. You will also notice that the materials used in these buildings all seem to be of some transparent material. Actually this is not so. I have purposely lowered your rate of optic perception so that you will not be blinded by the dazzling brilliance and radiance which is reflected from all of the buildings and streets which compose this city, just as in the mountain upon which it stands. However, you will be able to see enough of the brilliance and color so that an adequate description can be written.

In one of my previous discussions I spoke of rainfall. However, rain falls only in the lower plains. We do not from necessity construct our buildings with the thought of protection from disturbance of the elements. Rather, our buildings are constructed, not with machinery or tools, but with the creative energies from our minds. These homes and buildings therefore represent our first major efforts in the constructive use of energies. The earthman paints upon canvas the pastoral beauty of that which is about him. The sculptor may carve from stone that which he sees in his mind's eye. Likewise the bricklayer or mason is an artist in his own fashion.

We, here on Venus, are likewise artisans but instead of using the brush or chisel, or the trowel and hammer, we use as our tools our own minds, and the creative desires which stem from them, combined with the radiant energies from the Fountainhead become all of the things which you see about you. Yes, all of these buildings and all of the streets upon which they stand, and even all of the things which are contained within, were created by mind and not one finger was lifted in any construction.

But come, my friend, I will leave you here in the arboretum where we will again meet in one of the future hours agreed upon by us. May your sleep be light and untroubled.

Brother — Mal Var.

CHAPTER 8

Venusian Homes and Families

We welcome you back to Azure, brother, and I am very pleased with a number of things. Your continued and lengthy concentration has helped much in the continuation of our project. I see now that you are able to make contact and arrive here almost unassisted. I see also that you are beginning to expand your consciousness in your own inner eye to a point where I believe shortly you will be able to see everything about you here as it really is.

I had thought at first that it might be necessary to keep part of this hidden as well as to conceal you, as the strangeness and strength of this world might upset you. However, I am grateful for your many years of psychic work which will now enable us to progress more normally. I thought also that you might take a slight affront at being left on the door-step, as it were, while we were just on the verge of entering in and seeing what these dwellings are like.

But before we do this, let us ascend to the high balcony which you see on the spire above you—but we shall not climb. Instead, we shall use the powers of levitation. I will take your hand. See there, now it is done and here we are! Let us sit here quietly on this bench while you take in the panorama which is before you. As you can see, far out and below where we sit spreads one of the great valleys in which some of the cities of the lower orders are situated. In your earth cities the social structures are such that a man's place of dwelling is most often determined by your commercial system of finance or how much he has in a bank. That is why on other planets similar to earth we see such vivid contrasts—poverty and slums where human wrecks live out their lives in misery and want while their ragged children play in the street which separates them from their affluent and wealthy neighbors who live in great mansions and have far more than they know what to do with.

Such wretched contrasts do not exist in our cities on Venus. Even the poorest family or individual, living in the smallest dwelling, is far richer than your wealthiest baron. But he counts, instead, the richness of his many blessings, his closeness to the Fountainhead and his knowledge and ability to actively participate in the integrated functions of one of the great Spiritual Brotherhoods.

Around you and below you, you are seeing a veritable kaleidoscope and even with your still somewhat limited concept, this riot of color is almost unbearable. You are having a sensation which is somewhat like coming out of a darkened room into the bright sunlight. I will attempt to describe for your fellow earthman something of what you are witnessing. As you see from our vantage point, the city has only two main thoroughfares which cross each other at right angles. This is done to properly intersect the parallax of the magnetic lines of force. At their point of conjunction the huge dome-like structure of crystal which seems to be glowing in all colors of the rainbow is the central temple which we may enter later on.

I might say first that the cause, partially at least, of the reflection and refraction which seems to come from everywhere is actually a part of the function of the crystal-like substances of which all the vast numbers of buildings that you see before you are made.

From up here they present an amazing and intricate array of domes, minarets and spires; balconies and galleries sweep around the sides in many places like the one we are sitting in, festooned with an infinite number and variety of plants and blossoms. A little later you will see that in the various rooms and halls of these dwellings are also displays of flowers which could be an earth horticulturist's paradise. You will notice also that there are no windows in any of these dwellings. Ventilation is, of course, for other purposes than for ourselves, as we do not breathe in the manner to which you are accustomed. Your bodies need oxygen as a means of combustion. You might say your bodies are actually internal combustion engines and, in a sense, function much the same as your automobile. Here, however, our body needs are not supplied from external sources of food and oxygen, but come from radiant energy from the inner consciousness.

You will see also as we progress through one of these homes that the crystal walls and ceilings seem to diffuse a different intensity and quality of light. There is a reason for this. If you remember a number of earth-years back at the beginning of the radio age, almost everyone who first obtained a radio had one which was called a crystal set. The music which came through the head-phones was made possible by the rectifying properties of a small bit of galena crystal.

Your scientist of today knows many more of the amazing properties of the crystal. Certain crystals enable him to send hundreds of messages over a single conductor simultaneously. Activated crystals also make possible a new vibrant energy therapy which uses high frequency energy pulsations as the energy source. We likewise here on Venus in constructing these crystal walls and roofs have endowed them with certain properties. If you think for a moment that, like on your earth where you may have many thousands of different radio and television programs which are pulsating through the air simultaneously, it is just the same here except that instead of radio and television stations we have countless thought-form wave trains which stem from individuals or collective masses, from not only the minds of the lower orders of human life which reside on their countless planets, but we have also the great Masters and Lords, as you call them, collectively and individually radiating from the higher planes above us. You can see therefore that in a telepathic process there would be a great deal of effort and confusion in trying to single out one or any particular group of thought projections.

We therefore use various rooms and halls as centers of meditation where we can receive a certain narrow or limited band of frequency or spectra which contains only one or a few thought train vibrations of the individual or group we wish to communicate with. This function of rectification and separation is performed by these crystal-like walls and roofs and sitting in different positions about a certain room we can, in our meditation, engage in mental communication with any or all individuals of the great Celestial Universe who are capable of thought transmission.

As you will notice, even a single home or dwelling appears to be of vast and tremendous size. This is quite true. A single home may often contain as many as a thousand persons. While we speak of each other as a family, brother and sister, or father and mother, yet there are no actual blood ties as I have explained. Birth with us is materialization.

The question of family relation resolves into one of harmonic relationship. If I can again use a familiar reference, it is like a chord on a piano keyboard. Therefore, while there may be as many as a thousand dwelling in the multitude of rooms and halls which we call home, it is done with the utmost harmony and love.

Thousands of years ago when each of us first began to assume a small portion of self-mastery, we eliminated through our numerous reincarnations, one by one and step by step, all of the selfish, grasping attitudes which the average lower order of earth people seem to find necessary for their daily existence and, as these were eliminated, we replaced them with the pure spiritual attributes of spiritual understanding in all our relationships with the great brotherhood of man.

Now I can see this is a good place for us to return to our respective positions and rest awhile until we again resume where we are leaving off. May I say, keep us in your thoughts as much as possible. Remember that we here on Venus are constantly radiating our strongest thoughts to our beloved sister who is so patiently performing the task of writing this narration that she may not be troubled by discontinuance, for our brother is a missionary to the earth plane to help in opening the doorway which will admit mankind into the new era of spiritual prosperity; one which will encompass not only your earth plane but also countless planets throughout this great Celestial Universe.

And so to our brother and sister, may the richest of God's blessings be with you.

Brother — Mal Var

CHAPTER 9

The Still Small Voice of Spirit

A pleasant day to you, brother and sister. Since terminating our last visit which took place high above the city on a balcony, there have been some new and important thought questions which I have intercepted and which I would like, if I can, to clear up for you.

Some time after the close of this last visit some words were read from a magazine which dealt with relativity of various kinds of what the earth scientist calls factors. He has found that the speed of light and the pull of gravity, radio waves and such kindred and allied expressions have one common denominator relative to their speed in their, shall I say, expression or flow through this third dimension.

Regarding this factor of relationship he is still very much puzzled. It has not yet occurred to him that this 186,000 miles per second speed is only an indication, or as your doctor says, a symptom. The scientist has not yet pierced far enough beyond his limited finite concept to visualize that such expressions of energy, whether they relate either to the speed of light or electrical impulses or even to what he calls mass, would not and could not be expressed in his third dimensional world unless they existed first in some form or relationship in all other dimensions. It can truly be said that this earth world is only one of the many countless outlets and expressions of the Cosmic Fountainhead. All expressions of mass and energy must of course be logically expressed from this Fountainhead before they can materialize or assume some proportion or value in his world.

In short, whatever man does on his earth plane, or has done, or will do, and it makes no difference whatever the act or circumstance, he has first merely brought into actual continuity any and all of such things directly from the Fountainhead. If he presses the key on the telegraph or talks through a microphone across the world, he will have first pressed the key at the Fountainhead, or he will have spoken through the microphone from the Fountainhead. In other words, you don't get something from nothing. All of the something's which you call energy and mass had to first come from somewhere; they had to exist somewhere. This somewhere is the Fountainhead, which you earth people have called God.

As I have said, God is Infinite and in order for Him to be Infinite, that Infinity must be expressed in the finite. It must become negative and positive. It must become truth and error. It must be good and evil. Only in your association with this Infinite God you contrived to place the stigma of self and with this selfhood or ego, you have warped and distorted these infinite and finite conceptions into thought patterns which will take you thousands of years to eradicate. At no place and at no time will man come into the true perspective of his relationship with the Infinite God until he has eradicated the stigma of self and replaced it with the expression of the Infinite God.

Therefore, dear ones, listen not to the confusion of voices which is going on around you. How can anyone, in a world which is so filled with frustration and fear, with sin and negation, teach you anything beyond the realm of your own experiences. The outside world will give you nothing and teach you nothing. Their world, while it is all to them, as yours is to you, yet means nothing more than the ceaseless beat of waves upon the shore.

Throughout the eternal time of your evolution, you will find that only one thing is consistent and valuable in this evolution and that is the part of you which comes from the Fountainhead—that part of you which you call "the still small voice".

It is this Infinite part in its Infinite expression outwardly which becomes all the things that you are, that places you in all of the dimensions and realms through which you will progress; for only by the actual experience and the expression of experience will you come to know the personal nature, as will you come to know the infinite aspects of this God-self.

A little later on we will resume our narration and visit in the Venusian city of Azure, but for now, peace be with you.

CHAPTER 10

Helpers to Humanity

I am hoping that my last discourse did not take you by surprise or that you feel at a loss at my deviation from our true course; however, it is not often that the opportunity of the written word presents itself in our expression toward the earth peoples. While my discussion seemed somewhat short, it need not have been so. I could go on for many hours along such similar lines, and while we here on Venus do not pretend to be the ultimate in all understanding for we know of much higher and greater wisdom, yet all of such things must be added to the consciousness of each individual in proportion to his capacity for assimilation.

We do feel quite strongly about the blind philosophies of your many earth lives and I am not singling out your own particular earth planet. To us there are some similarities in such earth-life philosophy which remind us of litters of newly-born animals, huddling together for warmth and security in the absence of the mother. Many times some earthman, in the extremes of his feelings of want and insecurity and of his selfhood, has donned a superficial cloak of political or spiritual leadership hoping perhaps that he might hide the running sores of his many frustrations and fears.

You earth people have an expression something

like the "blind leading the blind." It is the fallacious interpretation of the many values of life that man seems to think he will find in some other individual. It is such dependency for the interpretation of such values upon his fellow man that often leads the individual far astray. However, as I previously mentioned, your earth is a sort of battle-ground where you earth people not only fight out your differences of opinion, but you will constantly reincarnate into similar life expressions until you learn that the true evaluation of life and its infinite expression does not come from a false superstructure of a conglomerate mass of other people's ideas and expressions but rather, in the true values, which are only preconceived in their proper relationship from a universal and infinite conception. Nothing is more restricting or binding than a limited concept which says that this is so or it is not.

Many of the things which you will see in our way of life cannot and will not be perceived by many of your fellow earthmen because of such restricted fallacious attitudes. For instance, we have long since left behind the place where we needed vocal cords to make the guttural sounds which you call speech, in conveying our thoughts to our brothers; likewise the written word is superfluous. In our understanding it is the principle or concept. A few of your other people who call themselves mediums are also expressing in a relative degree a more or less one-way principle or concept calling it, as they do, psychic perception or clairvoyance.

We here on Venus have evolved to a point where concept has not only placed us beyond the need of such low orders of expression as word forms, but instead we have a universal and integrated concept which, when properly used, places us at a point of instantaneous perception with the all-knowing, all-pervading wisdom and intellect as it is expressed in the countless dimensions of the whole universal cosmos. If you pause a moment and think, and if you can grasp even one small portion of this idea, you will see that I am having some difficulty in expressing to you even a small part of our way of life and our concepts.

However, let us go inside this large building which happens to be the home of one of my brothers. As you noticed yesterday these buildings are all constructed of some crystalline material and they are in a wide variety with domes, spires and minarets, all seemingly merged together or interlocking with various corridors, passageways and balconies. The earth people might think this a bit confusing. To those who dwell in an arrangement of five small cubicles, or some such number, this arrangement is quite suitable for their mentality. They would of course be confused if they found themselves in a home which covered several acres or even several miles in which as many as a thousand people lived.

Many of your earth animals and birds exhibit in some form, a higher degree of psychic intelligence than that of man. The swallows of Capistrano return at the identical time each year from an unknown place. Many species of geese and ducks, yes, even humming birds, have been known to fly thousands of miles across trackless wastes to find at the end of their destination, as they unerringly flew, the place where they were born. A bat can fly around in a perfectly darkened room wherein wires have been stretched without touching any of them. Numerous other plants, insects and animals all exhibit to earthmen in their cycle of life some seemingly unfathomable expressions.

As we walk around in these various rooms we do

so with the full and conscious knowledge of where we are going and how to get there. In fact, we do not even have to walk. As I have said, each room is constructed and ordained for a certain specific purpose and it can therefore be said to have a certain vibration. To find this room, therefore, means to merely tune in, as it were, to this vibrational relationship and we are there.

As was explained, the curved ceilings were constructed of a crystal material for the purpose of separation of various wave train frequency spectrums. Actually, as you can see, each ceiling is composed of a number of sections of parabolically curved parts. These sections are all of a certain particular shape and in a certain alignment so that they will assume the properties for which they were designed. By merely sitting in various parts of the room we can receive thought passages from any part of the universe.

As our planet itself turns upon its axis like the earth therefore, each hour presents a different section of reception from the universe. We therefore regulate our periods of meditation in accordance with these time factors, something like receiving certain programs at certain hours of the day on your television. However, it must be remembered that it is not a one-way communication and by the proper usage and direction of the radiant energy from the Fountainhead through our minds, we can transmit and send back to the individual or group some corrective and helpful energy which will aid in overcoming any negative conditions which we have intercepted. This will explain to some extent how we use a lot of our time on Venus and it will be discussed under the heading of spiritual therapy and healing.

There are, of course, many other ways in which we Venusians often go off from this planet in a more personal way into the lower astral realms which are associated with the more material planets, for the purpose of helping newly liberated souls, or, as you call them, dead people, who find themselves in a new world. Several of your earth books relate experiences where groups of newly liberated men from battlefields have found themselves under the direct supervision of a Venusian whom they portrayed or visualized as some great and shining soul or Master. Actually, of course, looking at things from our position, we are not Masters, nor are we even close to Mastership. However, from your earth plane we may appear to be in relatively some such position.

Above us, however, using the word above rather loosely, are many planes and dimensions which express life in a much higher degree of concept than we do. We are on the borderline, as you might say, between something which might be likened to impartially realizing or conceiving in our life some previously conceived philosophies and idea associations related to the more physical or material planes; and, on the other side of our perspective is, as I have said, the realization of higher dimensions and expressions. Therefore, we still need such finite forms and associations as cities or dwellings even though they are in a much more highly evolved state of evolution. This also applies to what you call a body.

When you begin to see us more clearly you will see that we have a form quite similar to your own, there being, however, an appearance of transparent (golden) radiance. I might say that another man from another world other than your own who did not have a body like yours would upon seeing us, as in your position, visualize us as he appeared to himself. This too is purely a product of concept, just as speech, intestinal assimilation and other factors essential to your life, are actually abstract and non-existent.

Now I am beginning to see that this may seem a bit confusing to you and refer again to small doses. Let us wait again for a passing of time and, like the rains from Heaven which should not fall too copiously lest they should wash away the soil, we will return to our respective positions.

With Eternal Love,
Mal Var.

CHAPTER 11

Love in Action

We will dispense with the customary greeting as we have been in contact almost continuously during the past many hours. Yes, you received my thought impression quite correctly and you have been wondering somewhat as to the many buildings and the position of the planet itself, in its position of usefulness.

Venus is what might be called a mother planet serving not only the earth, but a number of similar planets in a capacity which is something like mother, nurse and doctor. Many of those who are liberated from the flesh in these various planets have, shall I say, escaped from one prison into another. Ofttimes the bond of flesh and other karmic conditions are of such intensity as to prohibit a free and uninhibited ingress into another dimension. Under such conditions a person will, when becoming discarnate and detached from the body, be in an extremely atrophied condition. They are more like inert plasmic masses of some nebulous substance rather than the true cohesive thought-form body or psychic body which would normally be theirs had they practiced an open-minded spiritual philosophy in their earth existence. We, and other workers from sister planets who are serving in a like capacity, form what you might call brigades or battalions and go forth and gather up these inert helpless discarnate entities.

They may be drowned sailors in some battle-tossed sea or soldier boys who have been projected with severe suddenness into a strange world. Many of them often go right on fighting an imaginary enemy and unless great care is used in making them conscious of their position, they may go berserk on finding that the moment of the much dreaded death has arrived. I need not go into too much detail; it is sufficient to add that your imagination can serve you best in picturing the countless and innumerable places and conditions in which we salvage this human wreckage. Yes, my friends, with the spare time we have gained in freeing our minds from the obsessive flesh we have much more time available and are much more capable of serving mankind in a capacity in which he could not often serve himself.

Therefore, in your trip through our city you will not need to wonder at the lack of superficial adornments, or the lack of conveniences which you have associated with your daily lives. You will not find bathrooms as there is no need to purge and cleanse the body. The all-intelligent radiant energy from the Fountainhead strengthens us and purifies us and fulfills our every desire.

In a broad sense, our dwellings are not a necessity and are not used in the manner in which the earth-man is accustomed to using his. Our dwellings are conceived and constructed with one ultimate purpose and their function is to help serve and fill our needs in the service of Universal Brotherhood.

Later on you shall enter some of the wards and see how these atrophied spiritual wrecks are nursed back to a semblance of health and consciousness. Generally speaking, most cases will automatically gravitate into the spiritual plane which best suits their needs and more often than not it is the leaving off place of their last spiritual reincarnation.

In speaking of this most important subject, evolution or reincarnation, we might liken man's progressive cycles to a winding stairway which spirals up into some far-off unknown place; he will, in climbing this stair, find himself in one-half of the cycle where he will look about him and see and live only among things of the material domain; then as he progresses onward, he will go to the opposite side of the stairway and there he will see all things about him which pertain to his spiritual world or consciousness.

A moment's thought will point out an obvious fact, that the more cycles or revolutions he makes he will, on the spiritual side, be closer to his ultimate goal; whereas on the material side these things will be increasingly further and further away. Should he however, at any time, lose the correct balance between these two worlds or dimensions, he will revert back and fall downward, creating what is commonly called karma. This merely means that he will again have to tread the same steps over which he formerly passed and under the same conditions until he corrects this unbalanced condition. It might be pointed out that he is very seldom, if ever, aware that he is re-treading a karmic path. God in his Supreme Wisdom would naturally assume that man should learn his life lessons unassisted and solely from the inward consciousness.

To those who may believe that reincarnation has involved inversions into the lower orders of animal kingdoms, may I say that this is not only fallacious but extremely dangerous. You may form a thought pattern which has the power of hypnotic adhesion and you may find yourself evolving into some such state of evolution, even though it may be a fixed fancy and is entirely unrealistic.

So dear ones, as you read these lines, you must fix the thought firmly in all dimensions of your consciousness, that reincarnation is a wonderful and a beautiful sequence of spiritual evolutions; and in its proper order, it will take you through all of the realms of God's innumerable celestial universes. The only price to pay, if you can call it a price, is the constant, conscious reality of God's presence working in you and through you, and so for this time, brother and sister, rest with God's Peace.

CHAPTER 12

The Diversified Structure of Venusian Life

Although it has been some hours since we had a direct transmission, there have, however, been several occasions when thought projections have existed between us. I believe that we left off in our last discussion with something about reincarnation. However, as this is primarily somewhat of a visitation into our way of life, we will first explore a little further into the innermost reaches of this large dwelling which was our original, I shall say, exhibit "A".

If you recall, we had entered the front portico or atrium and you were viewing the many and diversified forms of plant life which were growing around the walls as well as in a large area within the center. This large doorway where we find ourselves, as you see, is a large corridor or hall which is very wide and very high. It might measure something like 100 feet wide in your earth measurements, by about three times that much in height. As you see, it does bear somewhat of a general resemblance to the huge Gothic Cathedral in a French city named, I believe, Rheims.

Of course, there is a great difference in the material used in the construction, as well as in the manner in which it was constructed. There it was done by hands. Here, as I have said, our minds performed

80

that function. About every fifty feet you will notice a large column of pure white crystal which rises to the base of the overhead arches. It is matched by a similar column on the opposite side of the hall. The sections of crystal which have been formed between the arches are, as you see, mostly of pink shades which diffuse a somewhat rosy tint of light into the space about us. At your feet is a floor which is composed of a mosaic of hundreds of pictures, all done in such a fashion that they reflect the true dimensional effect. It is like walking on top of a picture gallery. The pictures themselves depict scenes and historical events which have been taken from real life on the various planets. All in all, a person could obtain a very good education by studying the many pictures which form this floor. They are all constructed of the crystalline substance. The various trees, houses or people are cast or formed within the depths, in a manner similar to the plastic ornaments on your table tops which contain roses or other objects.

Now let us walk down this hall and soon we shall see the central pavilion. This is a huge circular enclosure with a supporting structure of pillars around the entire circumference. It would be, in your earth measurements, about the area of a city block. The floor here too, is constructed of many picture-form mosaics. The ceiling, however, is different. Bear in mind the previous functions of these ceilings. You will notice that the crystalline structure forming the roof-sections are formed of a large number of parabolically curved surfaces, each one of which seems to radiate or diffuse a different hue of light.

This central pavilion is actually a gathering place or meeting place where numbers of my people, comprising the population of this particular center will, at different times and for different functions, assem-

The Central Temple of Light

ble for purposes which may involve large and concentrated projections of mind energies toward some distant planet which is in distress. The peoples thus assembled will arrange themselves under these various parabolic facets in the order of the frequency relationship which is most conducive to their particular radiating frequency.

I might say here that you earth people and those on other similar planets are not quite aware of all the factors of radiant energy which enter into your dimensional relationship. You have many people who believe in sun bathing; others stress great value on more moderate dosages. It is somewhat well known, fortunately, that the sun's rays can be quite dangerous in large quantities.

The earth scientist has just recently discovered how to convert sunlight directly into electricity through the use of wafers of silicon. I would like to point out that in sunlight there is much energy which exists in frequency spectrums of which your science knows nothing. Some of these radiant energies can be quite dangerous as they have their most drastic effect on the psychic centers. Skin cancer is easily induced by these frequencies. There is also a break-down in the tissue of the subcutaneous structures which causes the skin to lose its elasticity and to age prematurely.

We here on Venus, in the upper realms, know of these factors and living as we do in a more highly evolved state of consciousness, are therefore much more conscious in some ways of these frequency spectrums than the earth people. That is one reason why we have gone to such lengths to construct our buildings in this crystalline fashion. There are also other radiations which enter into the earth from outer space but as they are less dangerous, I will for the moment pass them by.

Now that you have looked around this central pavilion and have somewhat satisfied yourself with its general appearance, let us if you will, please sit here quietly for a moment beside the fountain in the center. I have been receiving a barrage of thought projections from you and from our sister relative to some of the earth transcripts relating to some reported visitations to your planet one particular case of which I shall mention, as I enter into something of a summary of what actually occurred.

If you remember, it was previously explained that there are many orders of existence on this planet. In the very lowest order, any person living there would have powers which the uninitiated earthman would think miraculous. Such a Venusian would, when appearing on your earth, on shaking hands with you, have that peculiar feel which has been so described in the case where a *Brother Bocco appeared on your earth planet and was later followed by his Brother. It was said that they sought employment in some sort of a publication house for the specified reason of being supported in their earth life and to this I do not agree.

Even the lowest order of Venusian would be quite capable of supporting himself, at least for several days, without aid. He would of course have to return at frequent intervals to his own planetary conditions where he could replenish and recharge his body.

Picture, however, if you will, the emergence of a new being on the planet Venus, even in any of the lower orders. We must assume, as I have said, that he is comparatively a highly advanced soul. Finding himself in this new spiritual environment and with such spiritual powers as thought projection, levitation, frequency alteration relationships and other spiritual-awakening stimuli, he may become imbued

84

with an overzealous consciousness to help his fellow-man in some lower order.

He and others like him, may form some group or even a community and in their combined mental attitude of helping some lower mankind, will consummate their desires on some other planet such as earth. They will usually attempt in some way to appear either singularly or perhaps en masse and by adopting various disguises will attempt to reflect, while they are on the earth, a consciousness of the wrong and sinful way in which these men may be living. Usually such efforts, while motivated by spiritual principles, are short lived and unfruitful inasmuch as these particular Venusians have not yet reached a place of consciousness in their evolution where they have the true spiritual evaluations. They have in some cases become overzealous and attempted to force, in some way, what they believe to be their better philosophy unto some less understanding man.

This, as we know is not quite right. It is God's divine purpose and will in placing man upon the countless planes and expressions in what we call life, that mankind shall learn of Infinity and thus become an individualized finite expression in his infinite relationship with the Creative Source. This can be done in only one way. Each individual must seek out his own pathway; and whether he takes a long time or a short time is of no consequence in the mind of the God force, the ultimate factor being that the ever-seeking, ever-wanting, a higher relationship must come from within the individual by his own will and desire. Each experience, each evolution, and the sum total of its experiences are of no consequence except that they have been expressions in which the individual learned something more of the Infinity and purpose of God.

But getting back to the experience of one of your earth brothers, I will not say directly that he did or did not go to planet Venus in the manner described. However, I will point out to you that while it was entirely possible in such a manner, it is of small consequence and, like many similar attempts to help the earth people, have always come to naught.

Such lower orders of Venusians would, of course, have to seek out earthlings who could be used for their purposes. Just as in hypnosis, all people cannot be hypnotized, neither could all earthmen be changed in their frequency relationship to their earth plane in such a way as to enable them to be transported in some such vessel to our planet. So therefore, these two brothers quickly found and singled out such an individual who was so easily altered for this purpose. As the Venusians had not evolved to a point where they had separated themselves from the idea that it was still necessary to travel through space in some sort of vehicle or, even if they had so disassociated themselves from such ideologies, they still would have found it necessary to use some sort of vehicle, for the earthman would have completely revolted as he was not sufficiently wise to know about such things as astral projection, as in your particular case.**

In describing his trip, he spoke of arriving in some Venusian city (and he attempted to give some description) in which he stated of the peoples he saw that there was a separation of the two sexes into different levels of consciousness or, as he thought, two levels in space. This is quite true in the very lowest order on Venus. These peoples have not yet quite completely evolved into the necessary spiritual relationship between the sexes. If you will refer to one of the teachings from the planet Eros (which you have received) in which it was stated, "The psychic body

86

consists, somewhat, of a mass of wave forms, the sum total being the spiritual counterpart of each earth experience."

As can easily be seen, with each day, each year and each lifetime, the addition of all these new experiences as wave forms projected into the psychic body will in time displace many of the older frequency structures. These older structures have also their own natural tendency to fade away as they can only be kept alive through the nourishment of memory consciousness. Therefore, as in these low order Venusians there are still psychic structures that have not faded away, which have in some previous lifetime related in a very strong fashion to sex associations. These people, however, in assuming their new mantle of spiritual knowledge and its relationship to their emergence into this new planetary way of life have, with this knowledge, a sincere desire to eliminate the last vestiges and traces of the lower earth-life sex experiences.

In the material worlds such as your earth, sex is a vital and integrated part of your lives. Of course, there is much false knowledge and many perversions in the expression of sex; however, it is often the underlying relationship which will bring out the very best in an earthman but, with the passing of each evolution, comes new knowledge and new relationships. On Venus sex is no longer necessary as a procreative factor. It must, like many other things, be displaced by new and higher relationships. In the separation of the sexes in this low order of Venusian culture, these people have merely attempted to eliminate close relationships and such stimulating factors as might arise in such close proximities. Now I believe I have cleared up to some extent this particular incident in question.

One thing more, however; I believe it was mentioned that an extremely hard piece of steel plate was easily scratched by the stroke of a fingernail. Earthmen are puzzled at this. They say it would have required 17,000 pounds pressure to do this; also some super-hard instrument. It is quite obvious how limited these earthmen are in their knowledge. May I point out that the addition of caloric energy or heat in sufficient quantity would have caused this same steel to run like water; however, the puzzle was that no heat was involved. Again referring back to our concept of frequency relationship. Brother Bocco simply altered the relationship of the metal in its atomic structure with its basic frequency relationship from the dimension in which it was energy, into the dimension in which it expressed itself as mass. The density or hardness of any such mass is merely the product of relationship with the dimension in which it exists as energy.

Now I believe that this is about sufficient for this time. Look about you once more and carry with you all the beauty which you see around you and, while you find this extremely difficult to describe in your language, may I say that this too is a concept which is a product of relationship with the Infinite Fountainhead.

On our next visit we shall explore some of the many wonderful mysteries of this beautiful place. I hope sincerely that I have made clear some of the factors which pertain to the evolution of mankind in its various orders which are expressed as life on this planet.

Your Brother — Mal Var.

* See "The Venusians" by Lee Crandal. — ** (Such as the process now being used by the channel in this work.)

CHAPTER 13

The Crystal Cities of Venus

A hearty welcome again, Brother and Sister. I see the temperature of your planet is rising and I realize it would be more comfortable for our transmission at this hour. I had hoped in the previous transmission to have included something of the abstract sense of concept. I have stressed concept very emphatically throughout our numerous discussions. It is the basic structure of concept which always relates man to his particular stage of evolution. As we somewhat understand the infinity of what you might call dimension, or time and space, it is therefore logical that an individual can occupy any one or a number of positions in infinity according to his concept. This concept is actually the proper working part of the thing you call faith. You must conceive the infinite nature of the multi-dimensional Fountainhead and of its infinite expressions before you can relate them to your own dimension and your own time. A faith healing is always an expression of some such concept.

In bringing up the case of the young man who made the contact with the Venusians, I did not do so with the jurisdictional attitude that he had or had not done so, nor must it be so misconstrued; or that I had, as you say, an ax to grind. Rather, it was used as a basis for evaluation in not only this particular case, but so that such logical reasoning would enable us to assume a better position of concept. Quite often and in fact, it is a general malpractice by which the lower orders of mankind are constantly deluding themselves by false associations and thought patterns which they have assumed in a reactionary way of life. We might say of the Venusian and the young man, that his experience will be as I said, as meaningless as a wave upon the shore.

As the young man was attending a medical college and was completely steeped in traditional earth lore related to the objective mechanism known as the human body, he was quite anxious to prove to the outside world in the most, to him, obvious way of rendering such proof. It did not occur to him that he had expressed an illogical sequence and that inasmuch as the Venusian did not breathe oxygen, he could not therefore maintain metabolism which is a part of your normal physical body functioning. The whole idea of metabolism in your body revolves around the use of oxygen. The assimilation of nutriments depends entirely upon this process. In analyzing the blood of the Venusian, assuming that there was blood and that it contained nutriments, how then could my friend explain the lack of oxygen?

Such an illogical hypothesis has, in consequence, defeated much of the intended good purpose for which this experience was contrived. It is quite true that the physical body, as it appeared, did contain blood and the various structures attributed to it. However, they did not function, nor had they any function. The Venusian, in materializing such a material body on your earth plane, would do so on the basis of his knowledge of your bodily structures. In his particular stage of evolution and with the net product of his intelligence, he would quite likely assume that such a relationship of physical structure was a necessity on your earth. And so, in his anxiety, unwittingly perpetrated some unsound aspects which are misleading inasmuch as they do not reflect the true relationship of this Venusian. As I have said, in the higher orders of concept your position in the innumerable universes and dimensions will be determined by your concept.

Likewise, all the things about you in their sum total, will be only products of concept. The naked savage in your jungle could not conceive your way of life. He would be confounded and confused by the multiplicity of, shall I say, 'gadgets' about you. He would be terror stricken at the roar and rumble of your great cities. Likewise, you would find his way of life intolerable. That is why any explorer, in going into the jungle, must carry large quantities of his civilized appurtenances, for he would die without them. But I see I have consumed enough time on this subject. Let us merely say that we must not be deluded by illogical conclusions which have happened in the lives of others. If we seek far enough, the Infinite God within us will give us the answers.

Now I believe my dear sister posed a question as to how our buildings were constructed. The word crystal or crystalline has constantly occurred in the description of this planet and its dwellings. So first, because of its importance, let us find out what a crystal is. Your earth scientist is still experimenting with many of the mysterious qualities which are found only in crystals. These structures always seem to have a predetermined and inflexible quality of intelligence in their reactance, against or with certain types of energy frequencies.

The earth scientist has learned that he can grow crystals in his laboratory in some large glass jar with the proper solution of chemicals and electrical stim-

91

uli. He has found a means to grow crystalline structures which best suit his need. The whole group classification of such crystalline structures, whether they are found in gems or any other manner or form, are in themselves, a certain type of a dimension. In other words, here again is the Infinite God expressing in a finite way. Another comparison would be to say that certain elemental structures such as carbon, in expressing themselves in a physical dimension will, as part of their reverse cycle, express themselves in a spiritual dimension and so the carbon becomes the diamond.

In our world and dimension we have learned how to direct energy in, shall I say, a crystalline dimension. In other words, as in our buildings, these structures are literally grown—somewhat like plants or flowers. In this case, however, the radiant energies are so directed and controlled by our minds as to become such structures. In the case of a plant, the roots take up water and other earth elements whence they are taken up by capillaric attraction into the leaf structures. Here, with the combination of certain catalytic substances and energies from the sun spectrum, they are converted into sugars and cellulose, this process being under the direct control and part of, the green life cells which you call chlorophyll. So we in a sense become the chlorophyll as we take in and direct the radiant energies, used and combined, which are found in the atmosphere about us. These are converted into the tiny crystals which in turn grow into larger ones and thus are so directed as to assume the shapes which are useful to us.

I might point out that there is a similar process in whatever other substances essential to use in our way of life. As you will see in the pavilion which is about you, and in all the radiant beauty which is reflected from these crystal structures, so likewise, while it may seem miraculous to you and your fellow earthmen, we can also look upward and obtain glimpses into other worlds and dimensions which are just as miraculous to us in a direct comparison.

In our next transmission, I will attempt to confine our contact to continued and factual viewing and a description of this viewing of our planetary way of life. I will remain in constant attendance until further contact.

Mal Var.

CHAPTER 14

All Venusians Are Light Beings

Greetings again, Brother. As I have seen your light flashing in my mind, I know that we are again in contact. Yes, indeed, you are right and I am glad that it is so that you are beginning to see much more clearly and, especially, my people.

I was with you when you were peeking in one of the doorways a short while ago and I believe that you are partially conscious of what was going on, as well as seeing those who were participating. This is the room, and you were attracted to it, I believe, by the soft blue radiance with which it seems to be filled. I notice also that you are seeing a number of my fellow Venusians who are seated around the room in meditative positions. You are also beginning to see my brothers as they really are; that they are appearing to you, not like yourself with two arms and two legs, neither are they two-headed monsters with many arms and legs—nor are they like anything else which may have been depicted in some earthman's imagination. Instead, you see them as beautiful, glowing bodies of light which seem to be pulsating and throbbing and there are different colors and quantities of radiation or light which seem to come from different places.

When your sense of relationship is fully developed so that you form a true perspective of what you call form, shape, size, or density in our dimensions, you will see that we will in consequence assume a proper relationship like in your earth world. In other words, the appearance of our bodies may startle or shock many eartheans if they were to see us so because of their firmly interwoven thought patterns and relationships conceived in their world. Actually, the many radiant portions and color spectrums which seem to come from different sections of our bodies, relate in their proper proportion to their own senses or functions in our dimension or world as your various organs function for you in your earth body. Thus you might say we do have organs, but they are radiant energy sources. A few of your earth people have a partial knowledge of this, as they often refer to them by the word Chakra, I believe; centers of radiation which stem into the physical body from the psychic.

However, getting back to the subject at hand which is this particular room, these brothers and sisters of mine happen to be engaged in the concerted effort of sending forth healing rays into a certain ward in one of your earth hospitals which is filled to overflowing with small children who have been stricken with that disease of ignorance which the earth doctor calls polio. It is through the united efforts of these brothers and sisters that we will help many of these children to walk again. Likewise will the moments of fearful torture which are ahead of each of them be lessened by such healing-ray projection.

I see that a thought has crossed your mind inasmuch as this room was, in a particular way, just a little autosuggestive of some of the seance rooms which you have entered in your earth life. It is fortunate that your own spiritual forces were sufficiently directed to steer you away from these practices. While I do not like to reflect criticism or appear jurisdictional, it can truly be said that such misuse and misunderstanding of man's psychic self is malpractice. It is pitiful to see thousands of fine, wonderful people depend on almost daily communication (through some medium) with their loved ones who have passed on. These are like small doses of some sedative, inasmuch as the individual becomes dependent upon the medium and cannot, and does not, face a more realistic position in his personal philosophy. It is a sign of weakness and lack of spiritual concept which causes a person to seek out such means of communion.

The dangers and damaging results are increased a hundredfold when other phases, such as materializations are entered into. Sitting about in a closed and darkened room a person will in his extreme anxiety, create such strong thought patterns of energy that he can be collected and entered into by cunning, conniving astral forces. There are very few people on your earth plane who have the absolute ability of distinguishing such subterfuges. Many times these astral forces not only will use the thought energies in the assumed form and shape and identities of earth people who have passed on, but often, in the case of stronger and more advanced entities will actually pose as Masters. May I say to you and to all of the people of the earth that no Master has ever appeared at any seance nor will he ever do so. The reasons are quite clear and obvious.

In an abstract sense, a Master does not need to appear to any person or persons for the purpose of impressing them in some way to live a better life. He does not need to do so. Masters would project through the person's inner consciousness. However, I believe the term Master has been rather loosely applied. In my understanding of Mastership, a Master is a Master when he is helping to direct and to teach large groups of individuals, each one of whom you might call a Master. In other words, you may have referred to us as Masters, yet we are humbly observant of much greater intellects who are helping to guide our destinies. Let not the word Master, confuse you. The word itself relates or is suggestive of some form of chained bondage. There is no chained bondage in our spiritual worlds.

Attaining the proper balance and perspective of the relationships of the many planes, results in a vast and integrated participating membership in which each individual is an active participant who rightly enjoys the fullest measure of spiritual companionship.

Getting back to the séance room, let us say in conclusion that with them, this is a cycle in their understanding and to all those who participate in this philosophy; that inasmuch as it has been formed out of the fear of death, so it will pass from them. Being born into new spiritual realms and concepts, you will lose this fear and insecurity and you will learn the true relationship and use of your psychic consciousness. I might add also that great harm is often incurred by the spirit entities which are so contacted. It is something like some great hand picking you up and setting you down in some far-off place where you had at one time suffered great fear and anguish. It is quite serious for many people who are newly born in some spiritual realm and are just beginning to shall I say, walk, to be again confronted with some tearful friend or relative who, in his fears and insecurities, has sought them out.

A true spiritual philosophy and practice of such contacts involves many factors of which you are not aware, as you do not have the proper sense of values and the relationship of the many astral worlds in which the newly born souls arrive. It is best, therefore, to adopt a more natural philosophical consciousness. We must know first, and it has been repeated countless times, that death is a word which means change and that your loved ones and friends do live, just as you will, until and beyond the place and time you call eternity.

Yes, brothers and sisters of the earth planes, you indulge yourselves in many interpretations of what you call spiritual philosophy. There are some who are attempting to teach others a perfect way of life and yet they, themselves, are no less fearful than their fellowmen; and their very teachings come not from the high places nor from the word of God whom they profess to serve, but they speak and read from books, the words of other men no less fearful.

There are altars of worship where they teach that the mere belief in God and Avatar Christ means absolvence from their self-imposed sense of guilt. Let me say friends, that the absolvence of sin and error comes only from within yourself and that you used a destructive way. Your word repentance means this acknowledgement and your salvation from this sin comes not from the priest of the Temple but in the lesson you have learned and from your firm resolution to do better.

You must know that this life of yours is contrived and fabricated of countless dimensions and evolutions and that each succeeding lifetime is so woven and fabricated that it becomes your spiritual cloak, and within its radiant folds you will consummate a lifetime, yea, an eternity of service to your God through your fellowmen. Look upward, my friends, always look upward; always live in the consciousness of continuity and acknowledgement of the Cosmic

Fountainhead. See Its waters flowing into you as these waters in turn flow outward into all things that you do.

CHAPTER 15

Masters on Venus

In our last visit, I made some rather strong statements. Since that time, I have been conscious of some chattering between you. I realize, therefore, that my statements could also cause even more chattering should they reach the eyes and ears of those more directly affected. I will not try to modify any of my statements. Be kind enough to me, however, to realize that I am trying to bring you an impartial viewpoint from a higher dimension and one which is based on much experience and fact. So I will repeat that no Master has ever appeared or materialized in a seance room. If by chance you know of some instance in which a Master supposedly made an appearance I would severely question the position of both the medium and the entity or apparition.

Now I do not infer that Masters do not appear. Likewise, I place great value and emphasis on the correct use and understanding of psychic powers within their proper domain. There have been several Masters who have lived on your earth in physical form. I need not mention that the one called Christ is the most outstanding example. Masters have also appeared in different ways and in some clairvoyant fashion to some of the more highly evolved souls who have lived, or are living on your planet.

In the Bible there are numerous cases. A Master

appeared to one called Moses and he wrote the Ten Commandments, out of which grew one of the oldest and strongest religions of your earth. After the crucifixion, the Master Christ appeared to Saul, or Paul, who founded a Church which later, through a schism, became known as the Greek Orthodox and the Roman Catholic churches. A Master named Zoroaster also founded a pure monotheistic belief. A boy named Joseph Smith saw a Master and, under his guidance, founded what is today a very powerful church in your America. I could go on and on. Yes, I could even remind you of your own partial transfiguration when the Prophet Elisha, who is a Master, appeared to you with a host of Angels. Needless to say, such psychic happenings to any individual personalities have a great and powerful influence which is usually marked by the appearance of some Spiritual movement.

Masters do not run around and appear at some person's whim or will in some small confined seance room. Theirs is a highly conceived way of life. Any movements and appearances which they make in earth-plane existences are always premeditated, carefully planned movements which have had thousands of years planning in their making.

There is, of course, some conjecture as to what an earthman may call a Master. It is usually safe to say, however, that they do not assume a strong personal attitude. They do not go about proclaiming loudly that they are so and so. If you remember in your experience that although Elisha spoke to you, He did not call himself by name. You, however, knew instantly who He was. I could spend much time in discussing the innumerable facets relating to darkroom seances. There are very few mediums in your world today who can continue in any prolonged séance work without suffering some very serious physical or psychic damage. It is not a natural state for any earthman to discontinue even temporarily, the use of his body. Even the most careful automobile drivers have accidents. Such accidents do happen to those who engage in conscious suspension, no matter how strongly fortified his protective forces may be.

There is a much wiser, and safer, and more natural type of mediumship—something which you call mental mediumship. Here the medium always assumes complete conscious control. There is less chance of a cleverly disguised entity gaining control. It should be borne in mind, however, that like everything else, mediumship should be gone into gradually. It should not be assumed in one lifetime but in a number of lifetimes. It must have a preconceived purpose, which will result in thousands of years of training until it culminates as a useful science on the physical plane. Such mediumship is often expressed in many ways. A medium may thus be a doctor, or an artist, or a clergyman; or she may be a nurse such as sister Kenny. Your own mind will recall a hundred or so such mediums. Is it not better to see the infinity of God expressed in a beautiful and practical relationship rather than hearing a few weak voices from some unadjusted souls who have passed on into astral worlds?

You may also question the validity of much of the material or teachings which may come from those you supposed to be higher forces. As I have said, the earthman has no criteria whereby he can distinguish to an absolute degree the authenticity of the identity of some entity who has entered a seance room. Many of the higher astral forces have comparatively great spiritual strength and understanding; comparatively, I say, to your earth plane and consequently can reflect many wonderful and beautiful truths; but like the lower orders of Venusians who have gone astray in their overzealous efforts, they too must find (referring to the astral forces) that the darkened room is not the proper outlet for any philosophy which might appeal to the great masses who may be in dire need of such truths.

I have taken up enough time in this discourse; in fact, I feel quite selfish that my entire series of transmissions were so occupied and, to such an extent. However, as you have surmised, besides permitting you to expand your own consciousness which must be done slowly, our exploration of Venus and our cities has a twofold purpose. You could not appreciate or understand our way of life without the proper mental foundation. You will be in a better position to understand many new and even greater truths which may come to you in future evolutions.

For the moment, however, let us relax and stroll down the hall and enter some other room which may contain some great mystery. Here at the end of the hall is a doorway which leads into a nursery. You are wondering, when I say nursery, inasmuch as I have said we do not have children. In this room, as you look about you, you will see large numbers of beautiful little bassinets which contain, shall I say, spiritual embryos. These are actually tiny psychic bodies, or soul forms, of infants waiting to enter a mother's womb in some earth at the moment of conception. Here you will see nurses, if you liken them to such, moving about and caring in various ways, for these embryo souls. While I use the word embryo, each one of the tiny glowing forms which you see on these silken pads is actually in some cases, a comparatively old soul. Many of those here in the room have already been through several births and several deaths. They are, as far as this room is concerned, however, people who have met with a sudden death or have committed suicide.

It is one of our purposes and functions here on this planet to rebuild and reconstitute such violently dissipated causations as, in such cases, there is a distinct damaging effect to the psychic body. You may also wonder that the entire personal identity of a human being could be contained in such small specks of light; but here again I must remind you of the word concept and the factor of the relativity of space. In a normal sense, a person who has not suffered a serious catastrophe usually evolves into a new cycle of earth life with a complete psychic substructure, this being the composite amalgamation of wave forms which relate to his previous spiritual and physical evolution.

However, the tiny discarnate psychic body which you see before you is all that is left after the needed corrective therapy has been applied. Do not, however, confuse this psychic body with the superconscious of the individual. The real superconscious of any individual resides in another dimension as an integrated factor with the Cosmic Fountainhead. The psychic body which you see is actually only something like a link in a chain which connects the physical individual with the Fountainhead. When you become acquainted with the true factors and ramifications which enter into understanding what I have just told you, it will be quite easy for you to figure out for yourself just what position any particular individual is in at that particular moment of retrospection. In other words, this knowledge will advance you, in some respects, to a point which is comparable to something like an adept.

I might caution you, however, and all who read

these lines, that the greatest respect and reverence for, as well as an extremely careful usage of this knowledge is imperative. I have long considered the advisability of giving this knowledge, in the written word, to the earth peoples, with the advice of not only my fellow Venusians but of those from the upper realms as well. I have decided to do so with two provisions: first, that certain ultimate secrets shall not be given to you at this time. I am referring to the direct knowledge which would enable you to change your frequency relationship. I have also enlisted the aid of some vast astral agencies which will do much to correct any misusage which might arise if certain persons who read this book would use it for their own ends; neither shall it be scoffed at or derided. May I say that any person who does so, laughs at God and at all of the creative principles of heaven and earth.

I have shown you this nursery because I wished to implant it in the conscious minds of the future earth-scientists who engage in corrective therapies which involve the human mind. After reading the truths which are contained in this written work, they will better understand, in the treatment of some unfortunate misalignment, that the patient can and often does incur his greatest distresses from some great negation in some previous life. We here on Venus do not have the power to remove these conditions, as this kind of therapy must occur only in a certain relationship and at a time when the physical, psychic and the superconscious are united in an individual and with the individual's full cooperation.

I feel that you will agree with me when I say that you have just received a very astounding revelation.

Until next time,   Mal Var.

CHAPTER 16

A Venusian Healing Center

A pleasant day to you, brother and sister!

Because of the length of our previous transcription, I was forced to terminate our contact before the subject of suicide had been adequately covered. Because of the seriousness of this subject and the large numbers of people who so terminate their lives, I believe it is well worth some additional time.

Using statistics which are currently available it is said that in your America in the last year, (1955) about 19,000 persons voluntarily concluded their own lives; more than 100,000 additional persons attempted self-conclusion in which, fortunately for them, they were not successful. Many of these, however, will make future attempts as they were turned back into society without proper corrective therapy.

Many of these self-conclusions were small children —young boys and girls. The cause which induced their willful action was extreme hatred, frustration and anger against the whole world and particularly toward their parents who, in their tyrannical dispositions, induced these strong emotional strains which caused the anger and hatred. It is no joking matter if I remind you of a popular song which was built around the theme of a young girl who, having such feelings of anger and self-pity, threatened self-conclusion by eating worms. And while this song may have been invented for purposes of amusement, yet it can truly be said, it was inspired from fact.

Most adults can remember, that as youngsters, at some time they thought of retaliation against their parents or others by self-conclusion. As children, or as adults, there are also numerous other causes for this action. A person may feel a tremendous loss at losing his position, or she may have lost her husband, or there may be an incurable illness; or perhaps some form of lethargic neurasthenia which has been induced by the treadmill-like existence of your civilized way of life. But whatever the causes, as they may appear on the surface, these can all be lumped together and called by one name: negation. Negation is also the primary cause and largest contributing factor in causing all the illness of mankind and I make no exceptions. I believe that this statement will be verified to a large degree by most of your competent doctors. Negation simply means a sort of pinching-off process or a misalignment, of the vital life energies which flow into the mind and body through the psychic body, and which come from the soul or superconscious which is directly linked to the Fountainhead.

You may think that the air you breathe and the food you consume gives you this energy but this energy could not be assimilated or converted without the dynamic intelligent life-energy which flows at all times from the superconscious. If you will mull this over for awhile in your minds, you will see the infinite number of possibilities and the many ramifications which are involved in this gradual pinching-off, misaligning process which is induced by negation. The act of terminating one's own life has very serious consequences inasmuch as when the act is performed, there is an almost total separation from the life-giving superconscious. Leaving the inert physical body behind, the discarnate entity quickly drifts off into some low astral realm. His thought body which is composed of the reflected energies of his self-idea or ego is quickly dissipated; likewise much of the adhesive continuity qualities which hold the astral body together as well as the alignment with the superconscious.

We often find these bits of human wreckage floating half-suspended in some darkened region. They are usually without form or intelligence and are quite difficult to handle as they may break apart very easily. The earth term of bringing someone home in a sheet after a serious accident might be applied to these cases. Very often we bring these suicides back with us in an energy envelope or shroud, or they may be brought to us for treatment. Many of these cases are treated not only here on Venus but on other planets or dimensions which may be more suitable for certain cases which require special therapy.

As you noticed last night as we were standing in the very large room which I called a nursery, the entire room was filled with a brilliant yellow radiance. No doubt you know that the colors you see are indicative of the purpose for which the room is being used. In the blue or purplish room, there were healing projections being sent out in which case the therapy used was in the ultraviolet portion of the spectrum and related more strongly to physical conditions pertaining to nerve breakdowns, such as in polio.

In our nursery, however, the radiance here is of a more spiritual nature and is being used in correcting and rebuilding badly damaged psychic bodies. As you see, each one of these is contained in a circular vessel constructed of crystal which I called, for want of a better name, bassinets. These vessels are all standing in regular rows upon crystal pedestals. Each vessel is partly filled with a soft energy mass, something like the ectoplasm which is produced in psychic trances in séance rooms. It was this soft white radiant energy which you at first thought to be silk.

Now if you will step closer to one of these vessels and look within, you will see a small densely grouped cluster of gem-like bits of light which seem to twinkle like tiny stars. If you had the proper power of conception, you would see that, like the more familiar earth atoms, these are all conglomerate masses or structures of tiny wave forms of intelligent energies. Each wave form and its associated wave forms carry an experience, or a series of such experiences, from the earth life of the individual.

The body at which you are looking happens to be that of a seventeen-year old girl who took her life about 500 years ago. She is waiting until a suitable opportunity and for the correct time, which will be about 100 years from now, when she will again be born into an earth-life existence. I might say, however, that in any individual evolution, there are certain regularly spaced intervals between each incarnation which are determined by a certain law of harmonic vibrations. When a suicide is reborn into the earth-plane and again assumes the physical form, he will still be suffering from the effects of his previous self-destruction. It may take several earth lives before the full effects have been dissipated and until the psychic body has been rebuilt to its full strength. Looking again at the young lady before you in your consciousness, you do not see the silver thread which stems up into the room above you. This is something like what you might call a spiritual umbilical cord. Somewhere up in the room above, it branches off into

A Venusian Hospital Nursery

many little threads of energy which contact and draw in the radiant energies which are focused upon it. Thus the psychic body is kept alive and flourishes and grows stronger as she awaits the time for her rebirth.

Shortly before the time approaches for the actual moment of conception, she will be taken to the earth-plane and placed in contact with the aura of her future mother, which supplies her energy until she enters the womb. At the moment of conception the radiant energies which enter this umbilical structure, which you cannot see, are actually a form of the superconscious of this girl. Later on in her earth life (after being born) this superconscious will assume a much closer and more personal relationship; however, she may be somewhat of a problem child to her parents. She is quite likely to be ethereally-minded and do much day-dreaming and seem to have less cohesive relationship to her environment than is normally exhibited.

Although the room which you see before you may contain a thousand or more small lives, I can say that this is but one very small part of many similar nurseries, not to mention clinics, hospitals and rest homes of all kinds which are not only on Venus but on a countless number of similar planets throughout the vast number of universes. I will not attempt at this time to give you facts which may pertain to such similar structures and institutionalized centers of therapy which exist in some of the spiritual planes which you call the higher astral realms.

The bodies contained in this room happen to be only the very few which I and my brothers and sisters in this particular household can help. Someday you will learn and see a little more clearly, the importance of the law of harmonic relationship that helps to separate and integrate the many spiritual functions which you will find in your various spiritual evolutions.

So until the time when I can unfold more of these wonderful and mysterious facts of life, may we rest in peace.

Mal Var.

CHAPTER 17

Waking the Sleeping Dead

Again we come with our love from the planet Venus. I believe we were discussing the topic of self-conclusion and we had been in the ward where you saw a few of those in the suspended state awaiting a new opportunity. So while we are still on this subject of nursing, let us go into another section where we can examine another type of self-destruction which is a form of partial spiritual suicide.

We will re-enter the long corridor and pass over into the large doorway you see just before you; and while we are about to enter, may I say that you are quite likely to be reminded of some large hospital back on your earth-plane. There are, of course, no operating rooms where the physical bodies are dismembered and torn apart. Instead, we use our mind-forces in directing radiant healing energies; but see, you are in the ward. I see you are very much amazed at the size and large numbers of what look somewhat like the familiar hospital beds in an earth hospital. But come, let us step closer to one of the nearby beds.

Before you is a woman whom we shall call Susan. She passed from the earth life but a few weeks ago, and as you see, you would think her more dead than alive. In contrast to the pure psychic bodies of the suicides, the people in these many hundreds of beds

113

have all retained the semblance of their physical form. This is because in their passing, which was quite normal in most cases, they have retained in a somewhat shell-like fashion the hard thought-form energies, the word "hard" being a relative term.

Looking at Susan more closely, you will see she is apparently without life. Of course, she does not breathe because she needs no air in her astral form. You will notice also the grayish pallor-like color which makes her appear as if she were almost carved from stone. On earth Susan was what you might call an ordinary sophisticated, worldly woman. She had a business career; she smoked and attended cocktail parties and did numerous other things which are associated with the life one might normally find in a large city.

She did not have time, however, for periods of meditation. And if she attended church, it was only on special occasions such as at Easter time where she might show off some new finery; and while in church on those occasions, she was not listening to the words of inspiration nor were her eyes used other than in peering about the church to see what the other females were wearing. So the day came for Susan when she must leave her familiar earth life and the liveried chauffeurs and penthouses, furs and jewelry. While she did not willingly do so, her hour struck and she was forced to leave her body behind. Perhaps it was one of the physical conditions like cancer which caused Susan to leave her body; but whatever the cause, one thing is sure; Susan was not ready for her journey into a new world, a world which was entirely unfamiliar and strange, a world in which none of her earth things seemed to give her security and comfort.

While there is nothing wrong perhaps with the way

Susan lived on the earth, except that she devoted too much of her time and concentrated too much of her attention on the superfluous and often unnecessary appurtenances of a highly exploited way of life, because she devoted so much of her time and concentrated so much of her energies into the acquisition of those superfluities there was no time left to prepare for the future.

When a small green caterpillar crawls under a leaf and spins himself into a cocoon, it is because the small still voice tells him to do so. And during the long winter months, he will hang in a suspended state until the warm rays of the spring sunshine; then he will burst aside his little prison and will emerge a full-fledged, beautiful butterfly. Like caterpillars and all other creeping, flying, crawling things on your earth-plane, Susan too had a small, still voice but perhaps she loved more the sound of ice tinkling in a champagne glass, or perhaps the rustle of a new silk dress was much more musical in her ears; and so her time came and she was not prepared.

Do you see the little lady coming down the corridor? She is Susan's mother. She has been coming here daily since her daughter was brought here. Susan's mother lived in another age. She was brought up on a farm. She was taught honest toil and the way of life of her kinfolk. But no matter how many cows had to be milked, or chickens fed, or bread to be baked, Susan's mother always found time to steal away in some corner with the family Bible and there, in her quiet moments of meditation, she heard the whisper of the still small voice. And so when her hour struck, she did not come into her new world unprepared. She did not arrive in a helpless, inert state, more dead than alive; instead, she arose from her mortal flesh to her loved ones. She is living there now in a place some of the earth folks call Summerland.

As for Susan, it may be several months before she can hear the sound of her mother's voice. Perhaps she will be awakened by the soft touch of her mother's tears upon her face. Meanwhile, we here who attend her and others like her, daily and hourly project into her consciousness the ray of healing and love. We send her strength and wisdom; and while she is being healed, she is being taught the consciousness of her new world. She is being shown within her mind the beauty of the world which she almost lost.

Yes, we can walk up and down these aisles and look into the faces of countless hundreds which are like Susan. Perhaps it was not the rustle of a new dress which drowned out the small voice. It could have been an alcoholic stupor or a thousand other things with loud voices which are always shouting in your earth world.

And so, my brothers and sisters who are walking the many pathways of life, in whatever you are doing in those pathways, pause for several moments every hour and listen for the small, still voice. Perhaps it has been a long time since you heard it last and perhaps it will take many efforts before you will hear it again; but it is there nevertheless. It always has been, ever since you were created and it always will be, for the small voice is the God within you.

No, we do not use knives or instruments upon those who are brought here; only the radiant energy of God's pure love is used to fill the vacant places in their minds and hearts which were left unfilled in their earth lives.

These great hospitals, if you can call them such on Venus, have witnessed the scenes of many happy reunions of those who have awakened to the light of their new day and found the waiting arms of their loved ones. Yes, there are those, fortunately but a few, who do not awaken, nor will they; for in spite of all the love rays that we send them, they have in their blindness, refused all aid. And so they must wander in the subastral blackness of their own minds until the day comes when they shall desire to be freed. And then they shall pray to their God and He will send them a shaft of light; and like the tiny cocoon, they will burst the bonds of their prison for it is one of their own making and thus they will emerge into the warm rays of a new found sun, on a warm day in a new spring-time; and with their new wings, they will float grandly off into the beauty of the spiritual world about them.

Mal Var.

CHAPTER 18

The Psychic Body of Energy

Greetings and love to my earth brothers and sisters. In our previous transmission we had begun our exploration of one of the great wards where we here on Venus care for and heal some of the earth people who have passed into our worlds in a spiritually incapacitated condition. The importance of this subject cannot be overemphasized. I could devote many years of discussion to this particular concept without repeating myself. Because of its importance, I will continue from the place where we left off.

I have pointed out to you a particular example in the person of Susan. While all of the people who are lying in the many hundreds of beds which you see about you all left their physical bodies each in a different way or rather, from a different cause, yet they all had one thing in common. The one necessary and important ingredient in their lives was missing and that ingredient is spiritual consciousness.

I do not mean to imply that these people were willfully sinful. Most of the blame for the wrong which they did to themselves could be placed squarely upon the shoulders of an age and civilization which fostered such spiritual neglect. I might point out that in some cases the parents were largely responsible in not teaching a sufficiently strong spiritual attitude. So their children grew up and drifted into a material way of life. In order to understand more fully what actually happens when a person does not have spiritual consciousness in an earth-plane existence, we will first examine the psychic body.

I have partially explained this concept in a previous chapter. However, as we have progressed much further into our thought relationship, you will pardon me if I repeat some of this. The psychic body, such as Susan's or your own, is the sum total of all that you are, or all that you have been in any and all previous spiritual and physical evolutions. For the time being I am excluding the factor of your soul consciousness, as it will simplify somewhat our discussion. The psychic body, expressing the sum total of all these things and all your experiences, does so in one way. Each thought, each action, becomes a part of the psychic body as a tiny conglomerate mass of wave forms of pure spiritual energy. It is not like your earth electricity, inasmuch as it lives and is a part of a higher dimension. It is not dissipated by the time factor.

Now you may wonder how a man progresses. Let me say first, however, that this psychic body is not usually some shapeless form or mass of energy as might be supposed but rather, assumes the same form and proportions as your physical body. This is because you have a strong sense of personal consciousness. I believe your earth scientist calls this the ego. Actually, as far as the psychic body is concerned, it is simply the outer, shell-like covering, composed of energies which are coarser and harder because they are physical in origin. In the case of a violent murder, or where a person is very suddenly precipitated under duress into an astral world, he may be actually blown out of his hard, shell-like covering like a pea popped out of a pod. This shell-like covering which I call the thought-form body and its associations and origins in the physical world, will form a ghost or apparition which may haunt its familiar or material environment. That is why it is so difficult to salvage such astral forms, as they lack the adhesive quality.

This also is exactly what happens to a large degree in a suicide, but with this difference: the act of self-conclusion is one in which the person destroys his own thought-form body by a strong act of will which is necessary before he can go against the natural intincts of self-preservation. Thus you saw the residual remains of the psychic bodies of the suicides. Later on we will see other places where there are others who have lost their thought-form bodies, or envelopes, in different ways. In this particular ward, as with Susan, these are the more normal cases. Now I will get into the explanation of the construction of the psychic body.

Connecting up our thoughts again, we will see, under powerful observation, that these millions of tiny masses of wave forms appear to be in many sizes and shapes. They also reflect an infinite variety of patterns. Roughly speaking, we can divide these wave forms into two groups; those which were fashioned of negative conditions and those which were fashioned with positive conditions. They actually exist in two different realms or dimensions. The more extreme negative conditions may live through several spiritual and physical evolutions, while the weaker ones gradually fade and are replaced by others; likewise do the weaker positive conditions. In both cases, however, we must assume that the person is progressing upward in his evolution. In the case then of both positive and negative wave forms, the gradual fading and replacing will be done with stronger and stronger or shall I say, 'more spiritual' expressions.

Unfortunately, however, these strong negative experiences sometimes seem to form a core or nucleus which gathers about it other negative forms which will reflect as some diseased condition into the mind or physical body of the individual. This diseased condition can occur or manifest thousands of years after the original negation was incurred. Spiritual healing, in its true sense, means that a strong added outside mind force which is reflected into the psychic body, when combined with or added to the stronger or more positive wave forms of this psychic body, will rectify, or erase, these hard negative cores.

For the benefit of you earth people, your strongest and most powerful positive energies contained in your psychic body are formed in your meditative periods when you become consciously aware of God and the Great Creative Universe. And let your periods of meditation and contemplation be done, not in tearful attitudes of supplication which is sometimes called prayer, but do these things with the positive, powerful assurance that you can see and sense the All-pervading Wisdom and Intellect reflected in all things about you. This positiveness is called faith in your earth-words and is the greatest instrument which you possess to aid you in your many flights in your countless evolutions into eternity.

You can see now how it is possible to achieve spiritual progression by the constant rectification and the removal of wave forms in your psychic body; and do not forget that they must be replaced by the positive thought-wave forms which are: your acts of kindness and love, your feeling of spiritual affinity with God, your impersonal attitudes toward your fellowman. For you cannot give selflessly nor can you receive your greatest blessings in self-consciousness. Remember also, that your psychic body is you. Your psychic body is the vessel or body which contains, or is linked to the Great Fountainhead which you call God.

Mal Var.

CHAPTER 19

Astral Worlds
Their Nature and Design

I would like to continue, if I may, with another discussion which is very closely related to the nature of things which were previously discussed—that of astral worlds.

Every person on the pathway would like to know where he is going when he leaves the earth plane and that is only a natural attitude which is born out of the desire for security; therefore, a greater degree of faith could be expressed in each individual if he knew something of the place where he is going when he leaves this physical body.

You earth people have numerous, rather vague ideas and explanations of these places. You may call them astral worlds, summer-lands, or even heaven and hell, or purgatory. Other people have some vague idea that an astral world is something like a big shelf or flat place floating out there in space somewhere. If you remember, your history books tell you that a few hundred years ago people believed the earth was a large flat place which was pushed around the sun by an angel and that if you sailed a ship a little too far, you would fall off the edge. Of course such ideas are very infantile; likewise are many of the ideas of the earthman in regard to the dimensions which he calls astral worlds.

Referring back to our original concept of energy and mass, mass is purely a product of energy reflected from a higher dimension and by changing the relationship of mass to its energy source, change would also occur in its apparent density or solidity and with this change in density, there are also other changes which automatically take place. Mass will reflect or refract light frequency in a different relationship. Such a mass will also be more or less affected by other factors, such as time and space. This was what your scientist Einstein tried to explain in his fourth dimensional hypothesis.

It may surprise you and your earth scientists to know that there are other planets in this solar system that you cannot see. This is so simply because their relationship as matter or mass to their energy source is such that it makes them nonreactive to any of your physical senses. You cannot see, hear, or smell, or otherwise feel such a mass or energy in any energy relationship other than your own unless you are mediumistic or clairvoyant. I need not mention that this is the basis for what is called materialization in which a quantity of mass is temporarily changed in its relationship to its energy source, into your own relationship and thus temporarily, your senses will be reactive to it. It must, however, revert back to its original relationship.

Our planet Venus, occupies such an energy relationship with the outwardly expressed mass of the planet that it is much more spiritual in nature or, shall I say, more highly evolved; yet it still retains some of the qualities which make it reactive to your sense of sight. Your astronomer with his telescope sees it as a beautiful, globe-shaped mass of cloud-like formations. He has never seen the surface of our planet. He believes it to be slightly smaller than his own Earth, but this is not so. Because of the spiritual nature of the cloud-like masses which he sees, he has been unable to accurately determine the true size. This of course is of no particular consequence, except that it can be a strong point of argument with the many earth minds. If your astronomer could construct a telescope with which he could see clairvoyantly into the universe about him, he would see innumerable planets revolving in their orbits which he does not know are there, nor will he ever know in his present earthly consciousness.

There are such invisible planets in our own solar system that revolve around our own sun and use its energies, which are as I have said, energies which reside in another frequency dimension. With a moments thought, you will see that when a person passes in a more normal or highly developed spiritual consciousness, he will automatically be attracted to the particular one of these invisible planets which is most suitable for his present stage of evolution. When he arrives there he will not, as some people suppose, float on a pink cloud or play a harp nor do as described in any of the other foolishly contrived notions. He, as a more strongly developed person, will want to go right on living. He has, in a subconscious way, a strong thought pattern of previous lives and associations which are reflected into his conscious mind from the tiny wave forms which form his psychic body. He therefore will pick up the tools of his trade, shall we say, at the place where he left off on the earth in the earth-consciousness and continue on from there.

All this is done, however, with a much more highly advanced mental and spiritual perception. Actually he is learning, through these countless evolutions, the ultimate way of life. Gradually he will lose the thought associations which were born in the lower, more physical life which made it necessary, according to his concept, to express himself in physical ways. In his more advanced, spiritual evolution, he will form new thought patterns which associate him more strongly with the infinite spiritual nature which comes from the Fountainhead; and these expressions do not associate themselves with a physical form such as moving the arms and legs, or with speech, or sight, or hearing. Instead, his mind will be occupied in expressing itself in a more universal nature.

While he does not need clothing in the generally accepted way, he could, if he so desired, quickly construct any such clothing by directing energy through his mind. His universal sense of perception will supplant that of the five senses of his physical earth life. He will be able to perceive and conceive instantaneously and simultaneously, countless numbers of dimensions. However, this is beyond conception in your present earth-plane existence. I am trying to avoid any advanced, abstract evaluations. I know the limitations of the world about you and of the thought patterns which are formed by living in such a world.

In case there are some points in this last discussion which are not quite clear, I will explain them more fully in our next visit. So let us rest awhile in peace.

Mal Var.

CHAPTER 20

Return to the Fountainhead

Now that we have rested, let us again resume our quest into the infinities of man's evolution. In our previous discussion, we had emerged into something of the more abstract relationships. We had also gained some further insight into not only the development of man himself in his evolution but also into some of the new worlds in which he would someday find himself. As the Avatar Christ spoke, "In my Father's house are many mansions." So we have now found out that those mansions are not pink clouds, neither are we buried in some tomb, to remain until some such future day of liberation. In short, the more normal and natural sequence in man's many evolutions is such that he at no time will assume fantastic and irrelevant relationships with the highly ordained and conceived principles of the Cosmic Mind in any unnatural sequence in his evolution. He may impose upon himself certain restricted or destructive elements in his life and so express a retrograde concept of his evolution.

Generally speaking, however, we may assume that if a man is a mason or a tailor in this life, he will find himself in his newly-born and more spiritual condition on a planet which also expresses a higher degree of spiritual value. He will pick up and continue much in the fashion of where he left off. This is because, as

I have told you, his whole true nature of personal expression is contained in his psychic body. To precipitate him into some high, heavenly, state where all things were unrelated to his concept of things, and of what he is, would make him very distressed and unhappy. At some other time, I will discuss more fully the more retrograde factors which sometimes enter into an individual's life.

To you earth parents may I say, you do not create a child; a mother grows a body in her womb. In the science of genetics, it is supposed that all of the characteristics of the new-born infant are contained in the chromosomatic structures but this is only partially true. A child may, through such a process, borrow or assume certain physical characteristics of the parents but he does not in any sense borrow any of the spiritual. The spiritual factors are contained in the psychic body and in its relationship to the superconscious. You mothers, or mothers-to-be, are only the instruments in the progression of some individual. Your son or daughter is not the product of this generation, but has quite likely come through many such physical channels before arriving in your household. He may be even such an advanced soul that he may have chosen your particular household as best suited to his earth needs. Generally speaking, however, this is the exception rather than the rule.

A proper evaluation of earth conditions from some psychic domain in which the person may be traveling is almost impossible. He usually gravitates or is attracted to some particular household in a manner of frequency relationship. It is something like this: he may feel your vibration and the association of the many vibrations around you. In remembering that your child came from some other world or dimension, you must also assume that there are numbers of these and while some of them may relate very strongly to your earth world, yet beyond this, he may have lived in other worlds which were not so related. If you remember our talk on concept it is valuable only in a relative sense as far as your physical world is concerned.

In the abstract sense, abstract, in your way of thinking, does not exist. You have related all things about you and evaluated them according to time, space and related factors which deal with your own personal experiences. Thus you have created a world for yourself which is limited and finite. In the abstract, such limitation does not exist, as concept can perceive all things instantaneously. Of course, let me say here, only God is the absolute abstract; and as far as I know, none of us have achieved such perfection.

Getting back to the child and his relationship to you, you must as I say, remember that he is a product in a spiritual way of many incarnations and that he could have arrived in your home from some other dimension to which the present factors are entirely unrelated.

The many science fiction magazines that have been published and the many stories contained therein may seem fantastic as they are entirely unrelated to your world; and while they were all conceived as fiction, you may be surprised to learn how factual many of them are. All in all, they may be said to be an outward symptom of the inward self—of man's desire to free himself from the obsessive structure of material life. I do not mean to infer that your child who has come to you through this process of evolution has been some fish, or frog, or some many-horned monster which is often depicted in some of these stories; but only that man always assumes a relative form of body which will function best in the environment in which he lives. On your earth, there has been a cease-less struggle in mankind to orient himself into a phil-osophy of life which would adequately separate the true spiritual factors of spiritual evolution from the seemingly scientifically supported factors of material evolution.

Man's physical body is only the product of phys-ical evolution which was conceived in Infinite Mind as a vehicle in which he could best function on your planet; but it must be in no wise misconstrued or mixed with the spiritual concept. The only factors of relationships which exist are the preconceived associations which are born out of the experience of physical life upon some material planet.

This discourse, I hope, will begin your spiritual evolution toward your ultimate goal. For the one ob-jective which evolves from your whole or countless evolutions resolves itself in a personal struggle of each individual to return to the Fountainhead which has created and conceived him; and thus, in his prop-er relationship, man becomes an infinitely activated participant in the Universal Creation.

I will return soon.

Mal Var.

CHAPTER 21

Night Classes on Venus

Our love to you again, brothers and sisters. It has suddenly occurred to me that I left you standing in one of the healing wards of our city of Azure while I have spent some time in a somewhat lengthy discourse. Yet, if it seemed to be lengthy to you, may I say that I have touched upon a few of the more vital factors which relate to your very immediate future.

By now you may be thinking that we here on Venus do nothing but heal the sick who have departed from your earth plane or to otherwise help them adjust themselves to their new spiritual home. This is not true. We have another very important element of work which may be more to your liking. But in order to visualize its nature, we will again seek out another one of the great and mysterious rooms which compose this city.

Now let us enter into a room which is somewhat different from the two previously visited. As we step through the doorway, you see, and I believe you are quite surprised at what apparently looks like a large number of your earth men and women, each sitting at what very obviously is a desk which is faintly familiar and reminiscent of your school days. There are, of course, outstanding differences, such as the dome-shaped crystalline roof structures with which you have become familiar, which seem to fill the room with some particularly bright shades of green. The desk-like furniture is also different from the old, dark-mahogany wood structures in your school inasmuch as they, too, are made of some brightly-glowing crystalline material. These people, too, are somewhat vaguely different from the earth people whom you see about you everyday, inasmuch as they seem to have a sort of transparency and that they assume or absorb somewhat, the radiance which fills the room. Yes, these are people from the earth. They are the psychic bodies, the astral psychic selves of real-life earth people whose physical bodies are at this very moment in their respective homes, sound asleep.

These people are, at the moment, as you see them before you, being taught some of the more spiritual ways of life. In fact, many of the things which you have been shown, and which we have discussed, are being firmly implanted. In a few hours, they will return to their respective bodies; and in the morning when they awaken they will not remember consciously where they have been during the nighttime. I may say, however, that in the following days of their earth life, they may wonder at some seemingly strange things that happen to them which actually may be some of the truth or personal directions given in these night classes on Venus. They may accidentally, as it were, pick up a certain book in some lending library or in a nearby shop and in thumbing through the pages run across a paragraph which seems to open up a whole new world of thinking. They may accidentally meet some long-lost friend, who may start some chain of circumstances which shall also seem to cause some strange and incredible happening; but whatever the way, such circumstance seems to unlock a certain door which opens up a new world and with it a succession of spiritual demonstrations.

This chain was actually started and directed by what they had learned in these night classes. You, yourself, and sister Ruth have attended these classes. It might be said that sister Ruth at one time almost lost herself in a series or succession of such classes which lasted about two weeks. When I say lost, I do not mean to imply that she was in a dangerous position, but she did suffer a great deal of physical difficulty with some seeming lack of coordination. She must remember, however, she was actually directing her body through her umbilical cord, from the classroom to her earth body. Such a connection, which is sometimes called the silver cord, is always maintained by an individual who so temporarily separates himself in a dimensional way, from his physical body.

In case there are those who are reading these lines who might think this rather incredible, I could recite numerous examples from your Bible and other historical works or even cite true cases in your own time in which the persons involved had a complete and conscious happening of such astral flights. Many of the great inventions, works of art, poetry, political leadership or outstanding spiritual work are always related to people who are sufficiently advanced in their evolution that they take such astral flights into classrooms such as this, during their periods of sleep or meditation.

Sir Isaac Newton often sat for hours while his mind was in a far-off place, being taught the higher principles of calculus; and when he returned to his consciousness, he would proceed to rush madly to write it all down. Thomas Edison had a cot in his laboratory where, at almost hourly intervals, he would lie down for a short nap; and in such sleep state would ascend into some far-off classroom or laboratory where he would find the next step or the solution to a new invention.

As I have said, I could cite numerous examples; but if you are curious, you can consult the autobiographies of great men and women who have left something to posterity for their fellowmen. They always have some particular way of sleep or meditation for such astral flights into such domains either here on Venus or on the countless places of learning in some of the other higher astral planes which were most suitable for their purpose. You will always find in a close scrutiny of the lives of any truly great persons that all have found, in their own way, the key to their personal communion. Some may say that they are inspired purely from the Cosmic God, and this is quite true; for the Infinite God within you is always the causation for your best and noblest acts. Such personal relationship with God is always responsible for the greatest expressions, the most unselfish acts, the soft kindness of one man to another. But there is a definite relationship of this God with every mind in the universe and of any other universes or dimensions. The God within you will cause you to seek out the way which is most suited for the expression of Himself toward your fellowman. And while this may be a large or small expression of Himself toward your fellowman, yet each one is an important part of your life.

This God will also cause you to seek out others who may be more advanced in their evolution that you may gain new knowledge of expression in godship through this spiritual companionship. In this, there are no separations, for your physical world is only an outward expression for your true self. And in the countless evolutions which are before you, you will seek out newer and better ways of communion and expression. Yes, we here on Venus are a part of a vast network of spiritual planets, or planes if you would call them such, who are engaged not only in the salvage and therapy of human wreckage, but actively participate in teaching untold thousands from the lower earth planes; and while this number is small, yet each day the numbers are increasing, for may I say that, to your own earth, this is the time of a new awakening.

It is the beginning of the seventh day of the Lord as it is quoted in your Bible. It is the ending time of all the old prophecies and their fulfillments. It will be the time of ending for the cold wars and the spiritual distresses of the nations of your earth and while these changes may take place slowly, yet surely they must come to pass; for the hourglass of a new world has been reversed and the sands have already begun to trickle through.

In your future days, dear friends, it may be the seemingly unexplained happening or coincidence which will lead you into the spiritual pathway, or it may be that suddenly even more of the great abundance of spiritual blessings are suddenly added to you. Then you may be quite sure that you are, unnoticed by yourself, attending some spiritual classroom; and while you may not have the conscious memory of having done so, yet surely you will find that in manifesting the new way or the new abundance that you have been given proof of such attendance. And so for the moment and for the coming hours, may I see you sometime here on Venus.

Brother Mal Var.

CHAPTER 22

True Spiritual Evolution

A pleasant day to you, brother and sister. I see that you are still standing in the classroom which we visited on our previous occasion; and as there are still many important questions in your mind, we will also, likewise, anticipate those of your fellow earthmen.

You may have thought it odd that you found this group of earth people sitting at their desks, which were quite clearly molded after the pattern of the desks which were used by these people as youngsters. Aside from being utilitarian, the main purpose was that learning and being taught here on Venus would fill in some very obvious gaps in their previous scholastic education. Your earth system of education reminds me somewhat of a great sieve where the youngsters are pressed through and all emerge exactly the same size and shape. I am using this as the mental metaphor. There is a singular lack of proper education in the spiritual concepts. I do not mean the kind which are associated with parochial schools or any such theologies which are more or less orthodox. And while these religious concepts seem to fill the need for some sort of Sunday activities, such inspirational values as are thus incurred are quickly lost in the shuffle on Monday.

There is also a singular lack of recognizing the individual propensities of each child. While there has been some vague attempt to individualize the child, there has not yet been a constructive idea or movement to properly institute a spiritual educational system which can be combined with their other scholastic activities. Neither will there be any attempts, until such further day when the various sects and denominations quit quarreling among themselves long enough to form such a spiritual combination. I might say, this also would not contain the unrealistic and confusing elements which are contained in the expression of many of the denominations and sects. Such a program would have to be instituted and moralized by an entirely New Age concept—new at least to many of those who would have to support it while their sons and daughters were being educated. We, who have been on the path for a long time, know these truths and principles.

The other factor in individualizing a child's educational program is only crudely recognized by letting the child wander around the classroom, swishing his hands in paint or pinching a piece of modeling clay into some shapeless form. It is theorized that a child should seek out, in such a free expression, his latent talents. However only an old soul in a child's body could thus individualize his own strongest personalized traits. With the average child these traits are too submerged and interwoven with lesser traits which, when compiled together from such outside stimuli as curiosity in his new world, will often cause a child to seek out some rather strange and unrelated or even abortive expressions. No serious attempt is really made to direct his life expression or a vocational guidance until he reaches the last few years of his education. By that time he will have formed very strong and very definite thought patterns and philosophies. Under such conditions he has not the proper perspective to relate himself to his true purpose. He will often wander the world and his eyes fill with the dubious glamour of fame and easy money which he thinks could be his through some field of endeavor to which he is entirely unsuited.

He quite often goes through life in the pursuance of these false objectives and thus comes to the end of his days unsuccessful, bitter and frustrated. In escaping his physical body, he may after several reincarnations, find himself entering one of the great collegees or universities in one of the more highly evolved astral planets. There he will complete his education and his specialized training which will later on permit him to again appear on the earth and in his true expression. He thus becomes the great artist or poet or scientist. And in bringing to a full conclusion his rightful expression, he will have dissipated the heavy load of karma.

It is easy to see that a more logical course to pursue would be one in which the educational factors were included in each child's life which would enable him to at least start, if not fully become whatever it was that his Cosmic Mind had conceived him to be. It would only be necessary to make an accurate diagnosis of each child's potentialities and then institutionalize him through his educational period in what he was best adapted to do.

This is being done on countless other planets such as the one with which you are more familiar in your own solar system and which you call Mars. It is quite obvious after a bit of careful thought, that your earth-plane would soon be a new place with a new way of life if such a program were fully exploited; and it would save many people many needless reincarnations and thousands of years of time in gaining their rightful expression. Our educational system here on

Venus is not confined to teaching small groups in such capacities as would first start them on their right pathway. The people in this room are learning certain things which will be fitted in the proper place in their earth life so that by utilizing this knowledge in their future days, there will be no obvious deficiency of which they might be vaguely aware if this placing is not done.

Even the desks fit in with the scene. In this city there are many other classrooms as well as a number of auditoriums, all of which have functional purposes of serving the needs of different groups or intellectual strata of the lower orders of earth planets. Many of the higher Masters often come and give lectures and demonstrations in these auditoriums which are partially attended by numbers of earth people. These, of course, are the more highly advanced people who are serving the earth humanity in some great capacity. These classes have been attended many times by people like Sister Kenny, Florence Nightingale, Mr. and Mrs. Curie, Koch, Pasteur, Beethoven; in fact, I could name hundreds who come from all of the professions who are connected with the service of humanity. Many great blessings in the form of inventions or discoveries are thus given to the earth people, which has been partially made possible by attendance in these classrooms and lecture halls.

In the course of evolution, an individual in progressing upward, often attains outstanding scholastic achievements in one of the very highest astral planets and will quite naturally be interested in seeking an outlet for his best expression. He will be infused with the glow of service to his fellowmen. He will then reincarnate and emerge in a physical form in some lower earth order. Very often, however, the circumstances are such that, on finding himself in low order vibrations, he will be unable to express the purpose for which he came. In the seething unrest of his mind, he will send out thoughts for help which are intercepted by some of the spiritual entities with whom he is associated and who are working for his good and, in the interception of his plea for help, he can be led into a Venusian classroom where the necessary lacking ingredients of knowledge are placed in his psychic mind. Thus when he awakens in the following days after these sleep time courses, he will begin to find the way and means to bring into full expression the purpose of his earth life.

The earth scientist or doctor is trying to visualize that the seat of thought and concept lies within the gray mass you call brain. This is a badly mistaken fallacy. The brain is only an outward expression or coordinator of the innumerable life experiences of each individual which are reflected into it from the psychic mind. It is also said quite truly, that the average earth person, very seldom if ever in his earth life, reaches a point where he can think constructively. When I say constructively, I mean that he cannot voluntarily construct an idea or purpose without the association of his countless experiences contained in his thought patterns which are reflected from the psychic self. Any constructive thought must come through the psychic self from the superconsciousness. The superconscious is the part of each individual which, being connected to the Fountainhead, is the all-seeing, all-knowing, all-anticipating intelligence which sometimes trickles through the mesh of the psychic self in tiny droplets. Such droplets always are the originating sources of man's greatest constructive intelligence and inspiration.

Now the time for rest has arrived, so I will leave you for the coming hours. May you enjoy your earth life.

CHAPTER 23

Fallacies of War and Peace

Greetings brother and sister. In going through my previous transmissions, I have found that while I have covered many subjects, I have not yet discussed government and leadership of the nations of the world. And while we here in this city of Azure do not relate ourselves in our service to you in this capacity, yet it was deemed essential that this very important topic should be discussed.

Throughout the ancient and modern civilizations which have existed on your planet and these have been many and varied, yet in a broad sense they have all had many common basic elements and flaws. The theory of government is based on a natural desire of the many communities, states and peoples existing as a nation to factually integrate their many diversified ways of life into a harmonious combination with a peaceful expression of their life as best suits their needs. I am speaking, of course, of such forms of government as you call democratic, socialistic, or communistic. In the latter form, I am not referring to that great country across the sea which calls itself communistic but which is really totalitarian. I am referring to the pure and basic concept of government by the people.

Even in the past, history shows that while some governments were ruled by monarchs or emperors, they too existed as a byproduct of the people's will. Because the nations and peoples of your world as well as of other similar planets, have not conceived a way of life motivated by the divinity of concept which is contained in the Golden Rule, restricting measures are necessarily imposed by the proper functions of law bodies to properly enforce such restrictions. The peoples of your earth planet have not yet devised a perfect form of government nor will they do so until spiritual orders of concept are entered into. Many of your political leaders are motivated and sustained by high moral standards. However, due to the reactionary way of life of most of the people, the leaders too must participate in such reactionary policies.

This is one more example of the many kinds of treadmills the earth people get themselves into by dealing only with the materialistic side of their lives. They have not yet learned of a united and concerted spiritual effort of thought and action which would quickly dissipate the fear of war and political unrest.

We here on Venus do not sanction the use of the table of peace where the nations of the world are assembled as a place for strife and bickering. We do not condone the holding of the quill, which is plucked from the dove of peace in your right hand while your left hand passes out the implements of war; nor is any nation less guilty. While you are thus employed in scheming and devising ways to use your ideas and your philosophies of life in your peace treaties, your armies are shooting down the soldiers of another army which is likewise employed in scheming and contriving to force another idea of peace into your way of life.

Such fallacious attitudes of peace have bred new and innumerable wars, killed millions of peoples and decimated many nations. Thousands of such treaties have been written and even as they were signed, the signers were contriving new aggressions in their minds. You have, in the last years—and I am speaking to the nations of the world—capped a fearful climax onto the greatest catastrophe which has ever happened in the history of your earth planet. After years of bestial, bloody war, a new and terrible misuse of God's power was exploded into the world. In a few days, about one and one-half million souls were blasted from the earth or rendered helpless, while millions more were left homeless and in fear and trembling by this awful thing.

Now must all the people of the world walk this path of fear. You know not the day or hour when your world will topple down upon you. And even now you are in fear and trembling from the awful atomic weapons, yet you are devising new and more terrible ones. Surely this mad and awful race leads but to one place: oblivion.

We in the upper worlds cannot use strong enough language in our warnings, nor do you know the even more drastic effects which atomic explosions, whether thermonuclear or otherwise, have in some of the astral worlds. If you could but catch one small glimpse into these great unseen worlds about you which you call dimensions and see your relationship to them and how these atomic explosions were letting loose fearful energies which are breaking down and destroying many of the natural protective barriers between you and some of the great astral fields of negativity. If the leaders of the nations could see these things they would soon convert atomic devices into more useful purposes or quickly render them useless.

We in our position, working with all other spiritual planes, are doing our utmost to influence your lead-

143

ers into more constructive efforts at making lasting peace. As of today and this hour, there is a glimmering hope. The leaders of your America and of the great nations across the sea have been making a united and concerted effort to make this peace factual.

The history of the next few years will determine whether you are successful or whether your earth planet will become a blackened, decimated cinder. It might be well for the people of each nation, individually and collectively, to band together and put their last ounce of will and constructive prayer into crystallizing the efforts of your leaders.

You in America are fortunate at this critical time to have genuinely inspired and motivated leadership. May I also add that the past leaders of your great nation are also behind this concerted movement for peace and should you succeed, your efforts shall richly reward you, for then it shall be that your nation shall enter into (along with the other nations of your world) a way of life which has been called the Aquarian Age—an age in which God truly rules the world through the infinitely inspired leadership of Him who you call Christ.

For this time—peace be with you.

Mal Var.

CHAPTER 24

Self-Preservation and Procreation

A pleasant holy day to you, brother and sister.

I will attempt to discuss in this transmission two basic and fundamental instincts of creation which have been implanted in the life expression of every living creature on your earth and other similar planets. These two instincts are self-preservation and sex. It is obvious, with a moment's thought, that I could devote a whole volume to each instinct. It is these instincts which often, in a perverted relationship, cause mankind his greatest sorrows; likewise, in a normal relationship, his most joyous and useful expressions. Many species of plant, insect and animal life exhibit strong and normal relationships with these subconscious motivating factors.

The will to live and the desire to procreate are the basic elements which make life possible for all living things to survive and multiply. The tiny ant or the honey bee are familiar to you all; likewise are the squirrels. They and many other creatures spend many hours in carefully storing a food supply against the time when there is no natural source. However, these creatures seldom, if ever, die of conditions such as heart failure, stomach ulcers, hardening of the arteries and other diseases which man inflicts upon himself in his perverted anxiety and fear for his security. While these two instincts are distinct and separate, yet they are closely interwoven and are always found in close relationship. It is these perverted instincts by which man has created for himself a treadmill-like existence. Do you remember the pictures of the ancient treadmills where a poor slave was forced to mount an endless chain of steps? This chain of steps was so geared that by its movement it would grind corn or pump water. Often the slave was forced to activate this machine until he dropped dead.

In your modern civilization this same condition literally exists for untold millions of people. The great masses of the population have created a highly competitive way of life and so each man goes about trying to wrest from his fellowman the necessities of life. He has found it necessary to contrive new and more cunning ways to bring these necessities to him. So with each passing hour more and more cleverly contrived ways are brought into existence to further exploit his fellowmen. Nearly all earth people have some vague notion that their material possessions and wealth are their security. Many persons thus acquire a perverted relationship and thus it is they may amass huge fortunes which, of course, do them no good at all. While they are reveling in their false sense of power and security, they are also stricken with the pangs of inner conscience.

It is the still small voice that points the finger of guilt. And so they seek to placate themselves by giving away portions of their superfluous wealth to various charities or foundations, or they may at the time of separation endow almost all of this wealth to such purposes and, while this is a good and noble thing in itself, yet always does this type of donor seek, in his false sense of security to perpetuate himself forever in the minds of his countrymen for with each gift goes his name which is firmly attached. He erects huge buildings which are called by his name or he may create monuments of stone with his image engraved thereon, thinking that he will thus feel more secure. It is quite obvious that mankind needs a new and stronger spiritual concept to supplant this useless unintelligent waste of life. It can be truly said that this sense of insecurity often directly has caused wars.

A moments thought on your part will bring to mind a great number of possibilities. Of course, there are many millions of your countrymen who have a more normal relationship. They try, in their own way, to adapt their life so that it will not entail too many of the superfluities. They also try to develop the spiritual nature within themselves. However, here again is the lack of constructive knowledge coupled with the inescapable pattern of your civilization; thus, they also have become slaves.

It can also be said that the female of your species appears to be more cunning than the male. It is usually the male who breaks himself down on this treadmill, years before his natural conclusion. He has contrived a vast array of chemical substances and adornments whereby the female decorates her person to further superimpose the false aura of glamour which is strongly attached to the sex instinct. And here again is a strange paradox. The males are continually creating new conveniences for their females while they, in turn, find more leisure time to devote to their persons. Their homes are an array of mechanical, electrical and chemical conveniences. And so with the ever-increasing exploitation and creation practiced by the male, he finds himself led further and further away from a true course in life. He has even invented a great system of laws and enforcement agencies which are designed primarily to circumvent his fellowmen from doing things which would be more clever than his.

So he has thus created a comparatively large group of people who indulge in malpractice which is considered criminal. In this he has found ways to circumvent the other laws which have inspired his criminal malpractice. You know of these things and call them by such names as gambling, horse-racing, sexual prostitution, various rackets which are sometimes interwoven with your politics. In getting into these things, even I would get confused. It is small wonder that your world is in such a state of affairs. I will not attempt to go further into this all-important factor or instinct of self-preservation. However, I would like to touch more directly upon the instinct of sex.

Here again animals and insects often express a more normal relationship than man; while it is said that man has a higher degree of intelligence, yet he seems completely ignorant of the more advanced psychic relationships of sex. He may know of the biological and some of the psychological aspects but seldom, if ever, does he connect himself with his many life relationships in past reincarnations. Thus in his seeking a mate, he usually follows the same pattern which is exhibited by the lower orders of animals. He or she will move around in their particular society until they meet one of the opposite gender who seems to stimulate their physical reactions more than anyone heretofore previously encountered. This seems to be the motivating factor in marriage. The very high divorce rate which, in some sections is almost one to one, shows how fallacious this reactionary and illogical type of marriage can be.

There are, of course, many other factors which may enter into such divorce actions. The whole of your civilization is quite conducive to all types of abnormal separations. They are all lumped together and found in the false superstructure which has been erected in lieu of a more basic spiritual concept. Very often two people who marry may have formerly been mother and son, or father and daughter, or they may have been any one of a number of combinations of such family relationships; or they may even marry from a psychic sense of guilt that they have wronged the other in some previous life.

To reflect a moment's thought into the possibilities of these factors you will begin to see how little the earthman knows of himself; likewise, you mothers who bear children. The child who comes into your womb is not created by you. You only grow the body. He has found through you, the doorway back into the world which may have been his home for many lifetimes. He has been attracted to you in most cases because of certain harmonic frequency relationships.

To those who have knowledge of genetics and believe that a child's propensities are contained in the chromosomatic structure at the time of his conception, may I say that this may be partially or even wholly true as far as the physical body is concerned. A child may borrow the dark eyes and brown hair of the mother or any of the innumerable configurations of physical traits from either or both parents; he does not borrow his spiritual nature—the things which he truly is.

However, to you who are parents, may I caution you that the factors of environment with which you surround your child may do either one of two things: they may warp or distort him or they may add to an often expressed spiritual concept which may have been the motivating cause for your child to come back into this world. So therefore, be careful; each

149

child is a charge who has been given to you by the Creator. Yours is the responsibility of stewardship in a young and formative period of his life.

He may be an old soul who has sought you out, thinking that he could find, in the outlet or doorway which you have created for him, the true expression and purpose toward which he has developed through countless ages. Try to recognize in him that he, like yourself, is an individual, divine expression of God.

You may not know in this lifetime that your husband or your wife could have been your brother or sister; neither will you know that your son or daughter may have been mother or father, or that they could have been someone whom you severely wronged, nor should you try to know. Your lack of clairvoyant faculties would prohibit any factual knowledge, and until you have developed such latent outlets of clairvoyant expression, let us instead pursue a more realistic policy in dealing with the various members of your household and your social structures.

Yes, even your friends may have been linked to you with family ties. Let us all, therefore treat each other as brother and sister. Let us see in each other that we are individual expressions of Infinity and let us all participate in this Universal Brotherhood and express our fullest measure of love.

So rest in peace.

Mal Var.

CHAPTER 25

The Evolution of Earth Life

It was quite obvious that the two preceding chapters, inasmuch as they contained most of the relative values of man's physical and material expressions on his earth plane, could not be given in their entirety in two transmissions. So if you will have the patience to bear with me so that I may point up and objectify the salient points, future generations of mankind will be able to find a much more peaceful and productive way of life.

I have pointed out that while many governments were primarily instituted and conceived with righteous spiritual concepts, such concepts will go astray unless they are properly activated with the correct fundamental understanding of man's spiritual nature. Such is the case with your constitution and the idealisms which were interjected into its construction. However, it is a mistake to believe that any man or group of individuals can properly execute and transmit such idealism into your way of life unless properly ordained for this purpose. There is in your government as in many others, a distinct schism or cleavage between the spiritual expression and the way in which the government is expressed.

The direction of any nation and the expression of the people thereof, should always be so constituted as to be the function of what you might call a priesthood. Several other ancient civilizations such as Atlantis, Lemuria, Egypt and many others have, at different periods, existed under such a governmental function as was expressed in the divine spiritual concepts of the Temple. I realize however, that your present day would express innumerable spiritual concepts in a likewise uncounted number of temples. These are all good and a necessary spiritual function in their own relative positions. Or should I say they are much better than nothing? Yet none of the spiritual concepts which exist on your earth planet today are sufficient unto themselves to serve in a direct capacity as a spiritual government of the people. Thus it is that you have come to great strife among your nations, for you do not properly understand your relationship with your brothers and sisters about your world.

Such a peaceful Utopia as you have pictured for yourselves cannot and will not be resolved from such wide-spread differences of concept. In a future millennium, as it is called in your Bible, man will eventually unite himself into a Spiritual Brotherhood. He will find that all peoples and nations will function quite properly under a spiritual leadership which is motivated by the infinite principles of Brotherly Love.

Such a government will be directed and expressed to the people from a Temple in which certain individuals will appear on your earth plane and these individuals shall be, as you call them, Avatars or Masters. Today each man and woman in your great nation and so likewise in many other nations, are all sending forth a united and concerted prayer, or a plea to the inner consciousness for a solution. And so God will thus send you one. It shall not come suddenly or with fanfare and trumpets but only gradually, as it can be assimilated and woven into the structures of everyday life.

I also pointed out some factors in your sex relationship with your fellow men or women. There is at the present time a tremendous load of guilt among your people which stems from the ignorant and unrealistic attitudes toward sex relationships. It is also a seeming paradox that while man tries to live a moral and somewhat spiritual life and build within his consciousness something of a balance in his nature and purpose in your world, yet as I have said before, such spiritual motivation often goes astray without a knowledge of the active working principles and their proper application.

In your world sex has become a malicious and openly perverted concept. There is a tremendous exploitation of sex in almost every walk of life. The sign boards and shops of your communities are crowded with displays of the almost uncovered female form, the full impact of the autosuggestive usage of which, is intended to attract the eye of the passing male. Such a practice is licentious and demoralizing. Likewise are all the fields of the entertainment world cluttered up with these autosuggestive sex malpractices. It is a common sight in many of your large cities to see a church alongside a rooming house which is devoted to sex perversion. If I can quote one of your earth adages, you are "neither fish nor fowl". While you cry for spirituality and a release from your fears and frustrations, yet you foster and nourish practices which are open violations, of such a nature that they would obstruct any spiritual help which might be poured into your earth life.

We here in the Spiritual Realms would like a little more cooperation. Be sincere when you pray to God and do not defeat the purpose of your prayers by indulging yourself in the negative materialistic perversions of which your world is full. This problem of sex and moral issues which are so closely related in your everyday life, will also be solved in a gradual manner in a future day when you begin to recognize more fully the latent unexpressed clairvoyant qualities which are a part of every individual's concept. You will also begin to develop a new science of therapy which will more fully utilize these clairvoyant gifts of more highly advanced souls. You will also be able to institutionalize within your hospitals and clinics certain vital spiritual elements which you call faith healing or spiritual healing, by consciously recognizing and fostering such an attitude which will bring into existence proper training and spiritual healing. You will thus find a tremendous relief and a factual cure from the pressures of ignorance and superstition which have bred these so-called incurable diseases into your way of life.

Such training and specialization, however, will also be a part of that future day and will be a functional part of that Great Temple which will not only guide the political destinies of man but shall also direct his spiritual concepts. For only in the spiritual concepts will you find the true evaluation and solution for all the ills, political, physical or otherwise, which have been so incurred from an improper concept of spiritual wisdom. It is my purpose in the creation of this book that these many factors shall be objectively pointed out to you; and thus may it be, that what is given here today shall become part of the spiritual structures for that future age—your Millennium, your Aquarius, your Utopia.

Mal Var.

CHAPTER 26

A Venusian Birth

Greetings, dear ones, and may I say first that something like congratulations are in order, as I can see that you are now viewing us in our proper relationship and, as a consequence, you will be taken to the altar room where you will witness the emergence, or as you call it, birth of a person into our higher order. She is a woman we shall, for convenience sake, call Orda. She comes from one of the lower orders here on Venus and she has been here and studied while in a clairvoyant state; yet today she will actually be given a body such as ours so that she may resume her life here among us.

Now let us cross over through the central pavillion of the Temple and further down the hall we shall enter the altar room. As you can see, it is not a very large room, but it has some differences which are worth mentioning. At the far end there is a raised platform which seems to be surrounded in a semi-circle by a series of crystal-like mirrors. These are about seven feet high in your earth measurement and resemble something like a multi-section screen such as may be found in an earth home. Their function is to help concentrate the mind energies which will be projected by those who actively participate.

Overhead in the ceiling you will notice that there are three large discs of crystal which are shaped somewhat like curved lenses. One is a deep blue, another is red like a ruby and the third is a golden yellow. They will project a multi-colored beam or matrix of energy into the area just in front of the reflecting crystal mirrors. There are also, out in front, about twenty feet away, a semi-circle of seven low raised footstools which are used to kneel on. Throughout the room, there is a beautiful intense radiation. The floor is also covered with something which could be called a carpet but is actually a soft thick sheet of radiant energy, something like the more familiar ectoplasm, except that it, too, is a bright golden color. In the rear of this room are a number of benches which are sometimes partially filled by those who are closely associated with those who participate in this emergence.

As there is some time yet before the ceremony takes place, let us sit quietly on one of these benches while I explain to you something more of the principles of concept and why it is possible that you are now seeing us for the first time in a true relationship.

The words concept and perception, in general, may mean somewhat the same thing; concept is associated in an overall sense with the eye and mind, whereas perception is usually associated with the more physical relationships. In some of our previous transmissions, there were several statements which I made which are apt to be a bit confusing. I stated that as you first saw us here we would appear somewhat as you yourself appeared to others in your physical world. Later on, you again saw us where we appeared to be like large glowing masses of light. If a group of people saw a thief fleeing down the street, they would later on all give a somewhat different description of the fleeing man. The principle reason for this should be more fully understood, as in understanding this

The Birth of a Venusian

principle, you will understand why the earth plane people are constantly deluding themselves.

The mechanics of seeing on your physical plane, are something like this: your eye focuses through the lens, the various light frequencies which are reflected by tiny light-sensitive cells mounted on the apexes of tiny rods and cones which cover the screen or retina at the rear of the eyeball. The light-frequency impulses are received into the brain at the rate of about 20 per second. Your brain must then sort them in proper order with other memory impressions so that they are properly placed or conceived and related to all of your past experiences of reception.

In most people, the amount of synchronization varies considerably. In other words, if the eye sends faster than the brain can receive and classify, an incomplete picture is formed. Later on the mind will attempt to fill in such missing portions of the picture. This it does by taking some portions of other pictures which were received at a different time; thus the person will vary in his description of a scene or episode from the description of the man standing next to him.

Here on Venus our perception and conception is exactly reversed, in a general sense, from that of your earth people. There, as you cannot see Spirit, the physical world is the most predominant so that you view all things physically. Here we view things exactly opposite. We see all things in a spiritual world and in a spiritual way. We can, of course, just as you do but in an advanced way, see into your physical world. You can clairvoyantly see into our spiritual world. That is why when you first saw us here, you would have of course, quite likely been able to see us partially in our, shall I say, physical bodies and your mind would automatically fill in that which you could not see.

Such a view process would happen in a similar way to any other form of man who did not have our physical appearance. Therefore he would see us physically, as related to himself. You must bear in mind that what you call our physical form is an advanced spiritual form, while it does assume a shape and form which, as you now see, is quite like your own. If you remember when you first saw Ut, that he appeared as a Golden Man. As you see us now, we are somewhat like that except that we are very radiant. We seem to be projecting from within, many radiant shafts of light of brilliant intensity and many colors.

Completely around us is a broad frequency band of many colors. This is the Aura and is much more intense and radiant than your own. In a general, physical way, we are about six or seven feet tall. We do not weigh because we are not affected by the gravitational field. Looking at my face closely, you see I have a high forehead and my hair comes to my shoulders. I have two well-shaped ears, my nose is straight. I have a well-formed chin and my eyes are very large and seem to shine or glow. Over my body, I seem to be wearing, as near as you can tell, a shimmering translucent tunic. In fact my face, as I do not have a beard, seems to look like several of the earth pictures which have been drawn to resemble Masters.

These descriptions as I have given them to you, and as you see them, are as near as they can be put into earth language. However, remember when you come over here in some future spiritual evolution, we may, at that time, appear somewhat different. I might mention that several earth-plane people such as I have described previously, saw us and the higher Masters as intense, white masses of fire. So, as I said before, concept is a matter of relativity in the position you occupy in your evolution. But now it is time for

159

the ceremony.

The benches around us have been filled as we talked, with my fellow Venusians. I will not attempt to call them to you by name, as we actually have no name here. Names are something which help to classify personality traits. Now there are seven people coming into the room in single file, being led by one of our very advanced Venusians (Sha-Tok). Now they are taking their positions and kneeling on the small stools on the floor. There are three of the feminine gender on the left side and three masculine on the right, with the leader in the center. Now you will hear some kind of a strange music which seems to come from nowhere. The people in the semi-circle have their gazes intently focused on the area just in front of the mirrors. The music now seems to be growing more intense. It would be difficult to describe these sounds, as they are actually made by energy which is being concentrated into intense beams by the minds of these seven persons. It is something like a peculiar whistling, singing or rustling.

Now you seem to see a shaft of radiant light building up in front of the mirrors. This light seems to be filled with tiny brilliant stars which are moving about and blinking in a very rapid fashion. Now gradually this radiant shaft begins to expand and grow larger. There is also an appearance of solidity which is becoming increasingly more dense. Now you are seeing a vague outline of a human form, slowly forming just as an artist might be sketching it on paper. The features of the face begin to form in their proper places. The arms and hands and fingers are also appearing. Now she is almost here.

As you see, she is a very beautiful woman and when I say beautiful, it is a spiritual beauty which surpasses any physical beauty which you may have seen. Her features are fine and well formed. Her eyes are very large, lustrous, glowing pools of light. Her hair is a tumbled mass of waves cascading over her shoulders. Her arms are slender, her fingers long and tapering. Just as we, she is clothed in a shimmering veil of light.

But now the process of emergence is complete. The kneeling people stand up. The music has ceased. Orda steps down and is welcomed with loving embraces into the arms of her new parents and her brothers and sisters. I, too, am overcome with emotion.

So for now, in the excitement of welcoming our new sister, may I say, until some future time, rest in peace.

Mal Var.

CHAPTER 27

The Multi-Dimensional
Nature of Life

A few hours ago you witnessed an emergence or birth of a dear sister into our plane of life. Now that she is securely placed within the arms of her loved ones, let us return to the street where you first entered, so that we may walk toward the central Temple which you first saw, although not too clearly, at the time of entering. As we pass down the street you will notice now that you can see that my fellow brothers and sisters are coming and going, somewhat in the fashion of earth people. In this city there are no displays of merchandise or any other particular sights which might be seen in your earth cities. As was first described there is a, shall I say, heavenly radiance and beauty which seems to come from out of nowhere. While the sun may appear or disappear overhead, yet there is no distinct separation of night or day, as our ability of perception does not depend on the common reflection principles associated with the physical senses. In other words, the absence of the sun makes no difference as far as our ability to see and carry on our way of life is concerned. Nor are we influenced by the regular cycles of physical depression and tiredness which induce a sleep state.

On either side of this wide street are the occasional and widely separated doorways of the different

162

dwellings which are, as you have seen, all made of a beautiful crystalline substance. Even the paving which you walk upon is such a crystal. However, let us look at the Temple which is now very close before us. As you thought previously it does, in some respects, remind you of the earthly Taj Mahal. The basic structure, all of which is glowing, white crystal, begins with a circular building of white crystal columns, each about twenty feet apart, as the building is about 500 feet in circumference. There are quite a large number of these crystal columns. The roof is a butterfly-shaped dome, similar to the shapes which are pictured as Arabian Mosques.

At the four different places where a street ends or points toward this Temple is a small circular tower which rises to a great height and ends in a similar dome-shaped structure. The walls and ceilings are, of course, all constructed of the white glowing crystal. Around the outside in a circular fashion is a large area which is devoted to the culture of beautiful plants and shrubbery with pleasant walks just as in your earth parks. In front of each of the four towers is a beautiful lake, the waters of which are the purest liquid crystal. Upon the surface of these lakes are many beautiful glowing water lilies, lotuses and other aquatic plants; around and about the shore and floating on the surface are a number of beautiful, highly resplendent waterfowl. Several of these remind you of your more familiar flamingos and swans which you have seen in your parks and zoos.

Here is a convenient bench, so let us sit awhile and enjoy the amazing beauty and splendor which you see about you; and while you are thus occupied, I will go a little further into some of the numerous facets of your earth-life evolutions. I might say before this, however, that there will be here in this Temple a ceremony in which one of our loved ones will leave our Venusian way of life to ascend closer to his ultimate Mastership. If you remember, the tall brother who stood in the center at the birth of Orda, he is the one who is about to so ascend. But we do not measure our lives here by the matter of time as you know it on earth. Rather, our lives here are measured as cycles. In fact, when you begin to understand in a more abstract manner, you will see that the Infinite Mind of God is always expressing Himself, both finite and infinite, in the manner of cycles and evolutions; and this is true whether it is man or beast, fish or fowl, insect or plant. It is a constant succession of an infinite number of cycles. Energy or intelligence always stems away in a cyclic or circular path from the Fountainhead. So it must return and then it will begin again; yea, even unto eternity and beyond.

I will more fully explain this, inasmuch as an explanation will clear up some of the mystery which is associated with the coming and going of the plant and animal life on your earth. You must know, that as a cycle is a circle, within the cycle itself are many smaller cycles linked to each other through a certain law of frequency relationship. In your earth life, you have found that it is a world of extreme and sharp contrasts. This is because God, in his Infinite Wisdom, has so conceived and contrived that you must always, through the power of concept, constantly add to, in a constructive way, all of the infinite things which God is. Thus you will return to the Fountainhead where you will again resume another group of dimensions and worlds, and so this process is repeated and repeated. That is why, in understanding these things, I am humbly observant of my position in God's Creative Mind. I have tried humbly and without personal feelings, to picture to you some of the similarities in your earth life which still link you with some of the lower orders of concept.

In your community lives, in your dependence upon each other, I have said that it looks like you are all huddled together for security. In your daily lives, sleep, work and sleep are interspersed by periods of feeding and caring for your physical bodies. Your cycles and periods of life appear to us, as I have said, like that of a squirrel which is caged in a circular enclosure and running around, just as you do, in repeating the various cycles of your lives. I do not mean to imply that you are animals, because I understand fully your position in God's creation. Rather, I point out these things to you as a means whereby you can begin to further your evolution.

As we are close to the subject of the animal kingdom, let us go a little further into this subject. You may have wondered, as I have said, at the strange appearance of familiarity of the plant and bird life, as seen in some of the species about you. The earth man has not learned to the fullest extent that all such things have their own position in the plan of evolution and when I say evolution, I do not mean the principles which were exploited by a man named Darwin. I am referring to a more advanced spiritual concept. You may have wondered, does an animal or a tree possess a soul? Yes, indeed, they do. They possess souls but not in the sense of your generally conceived idea of a soul. In the case of man, soul merely means that he is linked up as an individual to the Fountainhead. A tree, or an animal, or any other living, crawling, flying thing on your earth, as in any other material world, is also linked up to the Fountainhead; however, in an entirely different relationship. It is God's expression of the finite and the infinite. Because an animal dies, or a tree is burned or chopped down, it does not mean they cease to exist. They existed before they materialized into your world as idea, form and structure of the Infinite Mind. Because a forest burns, does not mean that the trees have disappeared. Likewise, in all other things, as God creates all things, Creation began; but there is no beginning of time, for the Creation began in God's Mind; and, as it was conceived, so does He manifest.

The disappearance of material or physical forms from your earth does not mean that God has let Himself be destroyed. As such physical and material expressions exist in your world, so they must likewise exist in a suitable form in an infinite number of worlds and dimensions. The forest of your world of today may grow as the forest upon another planet in another day. We can assume that each regrowth or reappearance of God, in this form, is also attended by and reflects a higher state of evolution. While this is a highly abstract evaluation, I would like you, in the coming days, to give it much thought. It will explain to you how plant and bird life can appear in a much more highly developed form of energy in our city. It will also explain what happens to your dear little pets. As you all are and will ultimately be, the sum and total of God's most divine expression, so will you find in your future worlds and in the higher astral realms, that your pets have followed you there. They may not be the little flea-bitten dog that was so troubled with distemper but, instead, a much more highly evolved image or picture, if I can call it such, of that particular dog. Of course he will be just as real as he was to you on earth; but in God's great understanding, as it is expressed in the law of attraction, if you love your doggy strongly enough and he loves you likewise, so shall it be in the future.

Each animal, each plant or tree, starts in its cycle

from the Cosmic Fountainhead; and in this cycle of coming and going, it is always the same species as its original creation. It only changes in its frequency relationships in the various planes or dimensions; or can I say worlds in which it finds itself. Always remember, however, as I have said, you are the most ultimate and most infinite of all God's Creations and one in which He expresses His fullest measure. Do not misconstrue me, brother, nor the things which may seem to you a bit harsh. Your thought patterns are very adhesive and sometimes a great deal of expression is needed to loosen them.

Each and every one of you on your earth-plane is a brother and sister to us and our expression of love to you is far greater than any measure of love which you have yet conceived. So wherever it is in your many evolutions that you wish a helping hand, your Venusian brothers will do their utmost.

With our love, may you rest in peace.

Mal Var.

CHAPTER 28

Psychic Therapeutic Science And Healing

Again we come to you with our love from Venus. Yes, it is quite true our sister, Ruth, has discovered in her own way, through her vision, that we are Shamballa—or should we more correctly say, part of Shamballa. We here in Azure are one of seven such cities and places. Each one of these cities is directly related to your earth plane in a certain separated type of spiritual service. We, in Azure, function with those who have passed on from the flesh in some form of maladjustment, such as the soldier boys and sailors, the suicides and murderers, and their victims. The other cities relate activities to equally well-defined fields of spiritual and physical therapies. It is my plan to go into these different cities and, just as we have done here in Azure, make an exploration and find out more fully their own particular capacity.

You must remember these seven cities are all on the same relative plane of spiritual concept and are not to be confused with our brothers in the lower orders of Venus. Sufficient at this time, however, of this particular subject.

While this transmission is worthy of everyone's attention, it is directed particularly to all earth doctors and their allied and associated sciences. You have in the past hundred years made many noteworthy and commendable advances in the field of medical science as it is related to mankind. However, there is still much to be done. There are many very apparent gaps in your sciences and philosophies. There is still a host of unconquered diseases. I could mention a few of these such as cancer, epilepsy, Berger's disease, multiple sclerosis, dystrophy, etc. Any doctor could add a long list to these. I may say to you truthfully, that none of the conditions will ever be conquered from the physical side of life. You who are medical men, have as yet limited yourselves entirely to the physical body and material mind. You have not yet realized that man is spiritual and that his physical body and mind are only outward expressions of the spiritual self. I will create for you an allegorical equation.

If you had been, long since birth, in some obscure, remote corner of the globe and were entirely unfamiliar with the civilized world and could not speak its language—if you were then transported to some city and set down in front of a television set, you would, quite naturally, assume that the pictures came from inside the box. You would have no way of understanding the concept of transmission of electrical impulses from the transmitter. You would quite likely, in your curiosity, try to tear the box to pieces to see where the pictures came from. This is exactly your present position.

Just like the uneducated person, you are still hoping to find the solution for the unconquered conditions in the human body within its own physical structure. You will keep on looking until the end of time and you will not find the answer in the body. As I have said, the condition so incurred is reflected from the spiritual, or psychic, mind and body.

169

Picture if you will, the lawn in front of your home which has a sprinkler system. When you turn the valve, the water spurts up through nozzles at regularly spaced intervals. This is the life blood of your lawn and it would die quickly if it did not have it. So it is, with the physical body. Each tiny atom that is the basic substructure for every cell depends on its energy source—not energy from the food consumed into the body, but energy from the psychic self. This psychic self is, as I have explained, the sum total of all man's many lifetimes. Each person or patient must thus be viewed and diagnosed, not as the sum total of this lifetime, but of all the lifetimes. I know this is hard for you to visualize but so were the pictures in the box for he who did not understand. Because you have no measurements or instruments which can determine a psychic self, does not mean it does not exist. It means that you are merely ignorant of the fact. I have explained in previous transmissions that the psychic body, existing as it does in another dimension, is not subject in a commercial sense, to some of the predetermined relationships which you have established. You cannot see it or sense it because, in your lack of concept, you have not developed the sensitivity.

Roughly speaking, the psychic body contains all of the experiences; the negative and positive conditions and all the other sundry happenings which have occurred in the individual's life for perhaps many thousands of years. These experiences and happenings are contained as millions of tiny wave forms which revolve in miniature vortices, which in turn compose, in a similar equation, what you might term the molecular structure of the psychic body. As you have all agreed that, generally speaking, all incurable disease conditions that reside outside the contagious

170

pathogenic realm are incurred from wrong thought habits, as the mind is only an outwardly reflected concept of the sum total of all experiences. It is therefore logical that such cures must come from within the psychic body. The psychic body is linked to the physical body not only through the mind, but similarly to your sprinkler system. You have a number of psychic centers, or contacts, in your physical body which come from and through the psychic self. These centers are located in the solar plexus and in the center of the forehead, or pituitary, the extreme ends of the spine, the soles of the feet and the palms of the hands, etc. These psychic centers reflect energy directly into the atomic substructures. This energy is the glue which holds the atom in an adhesive, intelligent pattern. The atom, in turn, is a miniature counterpart of the numerous vortexes of wave forms which are in the psychic self, except, of course, that in the physical body the atom is in a physical dimension. You have a basic understanding of what you term psychosomatic medicine. You believe that many of the small negative fears incurred in childhood became the nucleus for a big neurosis as an adult. This is quite true as far as it goes; it just doesn't go far enough.

Each individual must, in your diagnosis, include any and all previous lives. As you know, often in discussions with patients, if a certain negative happening of childhood has been recalled, a partial and sometimes complete cure is affected. This happens to only about fifty percent of the patients. If you could recall to the patients the negative happenings in his previous lives, you would get at least a 98 percent average of cures.

The therapeutic action which revolves around such a cure from a mental disturbance, has as its basis a very fundamental concept. Picture if you will, a circle and that this is the life cycle of the individual, and that at a particular point, the negation was incurred; if it can be relived or recalled in a mental way at another particular point of this cycle, it will bring into play certain opposing dynamic forces which will cancel the negative quotient of the experience. The two different points of occurrence and dissipation may be widely separated in the evaluation of your earth time, such cures or dissipations being more effective at certain relative points. These are, of course, factors of harmonic relationship

Now I know that up to this time no earth science of medicine or psychiatry has developed a doctor who can so diagnose a person's life. Heretofore such a practice has been confined to a relative few and in an occult sense. You have one outstanding demonstrator of clairvoyant diagnosis who lived until quite recently in your modern world. His name was Edgar Cayce. For your own benefit you would do well to read some of his many case histories. Here again, however, as he was practically alone in his understanding there yet has been no developed or general understanding in the medical profession, either of his work or any others who have so expressed themselves.

Let me say at this time that just as hundreds of years ago comparatively little or nothing was known of your modern techniques, so in the future when the ultimate solution and cure of men's illnesses is found, no longer shall practices be confined to the physical realm but shall be an integrated concept of physical therapy and mental clairvoyance. The future doctor will not only be able to diagnose the superficial physical manifestations but will also be able to relate them to all of the patient's previous earth experiences

172

which have happened in his many evolutions and lives.

I am touched somewhat with a feeling of gladness for my brother who is about to make an ascension and it is a sacred and holy occasion; one which we do not distemper with sadness. Soon now you shall enter in with us to help us in the ceremony where he will depart for a higher realm but, until then, rest in peace.

Mal Var.

CHAPTER 29

Spiritual Ascension and Soulic Evolution

My greetings to you, brother and to my brothers and sisters on the earth. I see you have already arrived and are sitting on the bench in the Temple garden where we had our last discussion.

While you have been gazing at the wondrous beauty about you, you have also been watching the numbers of my people who are going into the Temple, for the hour approaches midday when our beloved brother will make his ascension. You have already anticipated the identity of this Brother as Sha-Tok, who gave you a transmission in my absence. Because of your somewhat as yet undeveloped familiarity with our ways and customs, you did not know that his beloved mate who is our Sister Erza was also making the ascension with Him. While we sometimes enter into this highest plane of existence on Venus as a single individual, yet it is very soon that our true mate makes His or Her appearance; just as the birth of Orda will, in a few days, be duplicated by the birth of her beloved one.

I will not take the time to discuss more fully the relationship of the two genders, as I have already discussed this somewhat in a previous transmission. But come, the hour is close. We will walk up these

174

The Ascension of Sha-Tok and Erza

three steps which lead into the large arched doorway before you. These three steps have the meaning or interpretative significance of man's three states of consciousness. As the whole Temple is built upon these three steps, they reflect: first, the lowest step is the carnal nature, the second step is the mental nature, and the third step is the Spiritual. This is also sometimes called the Triad.

Now we will enter the doorway. We will step aside and pause a moment while you get accustomed to all that is before you. While the overall pervading radiance within the Temple is extremely bright, your eyes are becoming accustomed to it and you are beginning to see more clearly what is before you.

As you saw from the outside, this is a large circular enclosure and around the outside circumference there are three rows of benches. These are already almost filled by my Fellow Venusians. However, I see you are much more interested in the central portion. You are wondering at seeing something which somehow seems to remind you of an astrological earth chart.

The large double circle which is about 50 feet in diameter, is composed of the purest red crystal. This crystal circle extends above the floor by about one foot. Around the outside edge of the circle is a wide band of the purest white crystal. The division is further emphasized by what appears to be bands of a golden-colored crystal. At certain regular divisions, this circle is divided into an equal number of segments by a line of pure blue crystal. In the center of each section of the white strip is a symbol which looks amazingly like the familiar astrological symbols. This entire circle is the basic astrological chart of our planet Venus. The earth people have misconstrued the basic meaning of these symbols by referring to them as animals. This should not be done. The signs are symbols which relate to certain controlling forces by which the planets are ruled, something like the chemical symbols of the earth scientist.

Each planet has its own number of divisions. The earth has 12, the planet Venus has 13, and so on. Each planet therefore reflects in a direct proportion some or all of the elements of these controlling forces. You will begin to see that there is a reason why so much confusion exists in the earthman's interpretation of astrology. A hundred thousand years ago, or more, he was taught this true concept of astrology, but coming down through the thousands of years of time without the personal guidance of some of the more masterly Intelligences, he gradually warped and distorted these basic astrophysical concepts into something he could, in his earth mind, compare more easily; just as your earth scientist today knows very little about even the basic concept of transmission of energy from one dimension to another. He has been struggling for many years to evaluate the sun's energy and how it travels through the millions of miles of an apparent vacuum as heat. It is not heat, neither is the sun hot. As I said before, the sun transmits energy from one dimension to another, just as the wheel of your auto transmits the energy from the motor to the road.

There is, shall I say, a huge cosmic motor or better, a spiritual motor which is connected to the sun. How this is done I will not attempt to explain until you have grasped further the idea of dimensional energy transference. The energy, as it is reflected from the sun, is not heat or light until it comes in close contact with the earth.

There, in the strong magnetic and static fields and with the combination of atmospheric friction, it is

177

transformed into heat and light. All of you have seen a snowy mountain top; and while you were sweltering in the valley below, the snows remained cool and eternal. The farther you get from the earth's surface, the less and less is the energy transference. If you could go up far enough, which many aviators have partially done, the temperature would drop to below zero (absolute). Beyond the ionosphere, as you call the protective energy shield, you would have to alter your entire concept of the values you have assumed on the earth's surface. The earthman of today is planning space travel by rocket propulsion. He is trying, through the means at hand, to evaluate what the conditions of space travel will embody. He has many surprises coming to him but, may I say, as time is short, that he will never accomplish space travel until he has learned more of the laws of energy transference.*

Even your weatherman is amazingly inaccurate in his predictions. He has not arrived at the point where he can see that his weather conditions are entirely the net results of the movement and behavior of the extreme high frequency spectrums which I have called the magnetic fluxes. The weatherman should know that the weather fronts of high and low pressure are all induced by tides of magnetic fluxes which move in a vast array of structural lines, not only around his earth but throughout the entire universe.

Getting back to the Temple where we were describing the circle, you will also notice a large square cubicle which is standing in the center of the circle. On one side, which happens to be closest to you, is a series of seven golden steps made into a little stairway which connects with the top of this cube of crystal from the flat surface of the circle. Above the cube, in the center of the dome-like roof, you will also see that there is a ring of large discs of pure crystal, each one of a different color. Each disc and its color is directly over the symbol, in its respective segment of the circle before you.

Now the time of the ceremony is here, although there have been no sounds which you might normally associate with a large gathering; yet there still is an even increased sense of silence. After a few moments you will again hear some of the peculiar, very pleasant singsong music of energy that you heard at the birth of Orda. Now that you are listening to the music, watch in the space above the cubicle. You will begin to see what appears to be the vague outline of a tall flame. It is not a yellow flame as you might see on the earth. Now, as it grows stronger and becomes more apparent, it is beginning to take on a wondrous, beautiful radiance of countless colors. It has grown to the height of about ten feet. All of the minds in this room are helping create this flame.

There is also a projection of radiant energies through the 13 crystal lenses which are focused exactly on the spot where the flame is resting with its base on the crystal cubicle. Now the flame has assumed such proportional brilliance that you are almost blinded and Sha-Tok and his wife Erza have made their appearance and are moving slowly, hand in hand, toward the seven steps.

Sha-Tok is tall and straight. His hair, a flaming mass of gold, falls about his shoulders; and while he has been here among us for about 2000 years, his face is young and youthful. Erza, too, is very beautiful. Her hair is of a copper-red color. She, like her mate walks straight and erect. Her beautiful features are unmarred by lines of age. Both Sha-Tok and Erza have their gaze fixed upon the flame. They do not look around. They do not appear to be sad or frightened, nor are they. Within their minds are pulsating energy

179

currents of esthetic love. They are in tune and are part of the pulsating mind of God. And now the slow ascent up the stairway begins. At the top they pause just before the flame, then arm in arm, they step into its pulsating radiant energy and are gone. Gradually the singing voice of energy dies down and as it dies, so does the flame.

In a little while all is as before. Slowly my brothers and sisters begin their exit from the Temple. Their faces are not filled with sorrow. Instead, each one reflects some of the radiant beauty of the energy which they have helped direct. Each mind is filled with a new courage and a new measure of inspiration. Each one has rededicated himself or herself to his consecrated service of his fellowman, and so in the coming time, we shall not forget Sha-Tok or Erza, for they shall come again among us from time to time, though we shall not see them quite as they formerly were, for they have ascended into another realm which is almost beyond our vision.

Erza and Sha-Tok may come to us with others in our future days to teach new truths, to give us new inspiration and vision and thus, my friends, must you also do likewise. Know not the fear of that which you call death, for death is the separation of the physical consciousness and means only liberation into a higher realm; and with each succeeding graduation, do you ever approach and draw closer to the Fountainhead of God.

Mal Var.

*The mention of space travel does not refer to such nearby bodies as the moon etc., but rather, to other planets at great distances.

CHAPTER 30

The Seven Teaching Centers of Shamballa

Greetings again, brother and sister!

We here in Azure have been observing some hours of meditation and contemplation since the departure of our beloved Brother Sha-Tok and our beloved Sister Erza. I would say a word here, too, for she likewise has ascended in the seven evolutions through Shamballa to the Ascension.

As I have been looking in your minds and sorting out your thoughts, I see that you have been rather excited about putting together some pieces of evidence which have caused you to believe that you were the man called Jesus, who lived on your earth 2000 years ago. Now that you have come so close to the truth, I believe it is only fair to give you more definite information. I have carefully weighed and evaluated the chances of this information being a bit disconcerting to some of the earth minds who will read these lines. Yes, Sha-Tok was Jesus. It was not coincidence that you and sister Ruth were all part of a carefully chosen plan whereby we could clear up some of the mysteries of Shamballa, as you were both living in the Holy Land at the time of the crucifixion and, as you know, were very vitally concerned with the mission. Through your participation as a channel for this expression, it was much more easily accomplished.

You, as Jesus, at the time of his birth, came from the planet *Eros. It was this bright, very highly evolved planet which shed its shining rays in the early morning hours of the birth. It was on this planet that the Master Jesus went through a series of evolutions where He learned the secrets of higher powers which in His earth life, enabled him to perform the many miracles. As I have said, the Great Ones on Eros are quite highly advanced; so much so that they can guide their planet through the universe wherever they wish to go. There are, however, many abstract concepts in the evaluation of the various positions into which man evolves. These might be called Adepts, Masters or Lords. In the Infinite Concept, they are not so called but they assume a certain relationship which expresses its own quotient of Infinity in the whole structure of the universe.

We here on Venus who understand these truths, do not evaluate ourselves by assuming any position other than that which relates to our particular service to our particular planet. Thus it is with the seven cities of Shamballa and while each city has its own particular relationship and function in the service of mankind, yet all have the same general appearance. Many earth people, including a few who live in your modern times, have caught glimpses in psychic moments of these cities. So while they all generally agree somewhat as to their general appearance, apparently no one knew, nor were they given information that there were not one, but seven cities. In our explanation of Azure, we have seen only a small fraction.

As I have mentioned these seven cities which comprise Shamballa, it is also only fair that I give you more information. However, the subject here is very

*Planet not yet known by earth astronomers.

182

broad and could easily cover a number of volumes, but a short digest will give you something of an idea. These seven cities are functioning like Azure—in their own individual expression of their capacity to mankind, on numerous earth planets. The seven cities, while they are all on a somewhat similar spiritual level, are on seven different planets. These are spaced like a belt around our particular galaxy or star cluster. Thus they can serve not only earth but a large number of similar planets. There are other planets which also serve the lower orders of humanity with Venus and her six sister planets. Each has a particular way in which service is rendered. One serves in the field of philosophy. We serve in the art of healing and adjustment. Others serve in fields of political and other types of leadership; poetry, music and kindred arts, science, religion, etc.

As in other cities, we have large galleries with exhibits which depict the entire history of mankind in his evolution through the various planetary systems. There are also laboratories where a student can go and learn all the scientific arts which relate, in their innumerable numbers, to the expression of life on these numerous planets. It would take you many years to explore our city alone.

There is one more point which I would like to clear up in the ceremony of the ascension you witnessed. While it was performed in the large central Temple, this was especially done because of the high position of Sha-Tok and Erza. Sometimes, however, the ascending individuals may choose to use a more private way. They will thus make their ascension in any one of the small altar rooms like the one which we saw at the birth of Orda. However, in each instance of ascension, whether it is in the central Temple or in one of the small altar rooms, the process is the same.

Throughout the preceding chapters and our various discussions, I have attempted to give you not only a word picture of our planet and our city but I have also tried to bring you some of the more important elements which will enter into your future lives. Whether or not this will be of any value will depend upon each individual. In God's great universal world there is no one who will stand over you with a whip, neither will we turn our backs to you when you need help. The important thing to remember is that your progress or your evolution or whatever you get out of life, whether here or hereafter, depends upon your own attitudes.

No one with a closed mind gets very far. Your book of life is written with your own hand and all that you are you will see because they are the things which compose your spiritual body. It is logical to assume that these be of a nature which can live and function in a world which is a part of God.

It is with great reluctance that I must write the final lines and speak the last words which will bring this book to a close. Now I say to our beloved sister Ruth and brother Ernest, that you have indeed rendered a great service for which we are grateful and although these last lines are being written, it does not mean a termination of our contacts. In some future time, we will again return to you in this capacity and new volumes will be written as they are required by the seekers of Truth.

I further appreciate my own personal opportunity and that I was granted the opportunity to speak as I wished. If there are some doubts or questions as to any of the information, please feel free to send the thought and we shall add to or create new chapters, as you see fit. My only regret is that we could not further explore our city at this time but, as I have said, we shall do that together sometime, at some future day. So with all our love may you prosper and find the fullest measure of God's Eternal Love.

The Venusians.

*It should be borne in mind that it is the Higher Self or Super Self of the man Jesus, or Akhenaton, Zoroaster, Anaxagoras, E. L. Norman, etc., (herein called Sha-Tok), that lives in the Higher Worlds and functions (oscillates) through the physical mind of the earthman (Jesus, etc.), for no such Super Being could exist in an earth dimension—this, an abstract Principle, described further in other Unarius works.

These Visitations to other planets are continued in subsequent "Pulse of Creation" books, Vols. 2—5, incl.

ADDENDUM

A Word from the Channel

It had been my original intention that as a channel for this book I would remain unheard and unspoken. However, in view of two recent national announcements, I have been prompted to add or point up several of the more vital and pertinent issues contained in this book. And while these issues have been quite thoroughly and adequately covered, yet I believe what I have to say will not go amiss.

A few days ago, our Government announced it was planning to build the long dreamed of space satellite. They had hoped to project some sort of rocket which would travel in an orbit around the earth. Almost immediately, Russia also announced similar plans. It is quite obvious that while these two similar plans were loudly acclaimed as scientific projects inspired for the sake of pure science, behind it all was the same old militant ulterior motive. And so again it has come to pass that two nations are extending their right hands in a gesture of friendship and peace, while in their left hands they clutch the weapons of war. It should be equally obvious to the leaders of our nation that after thousands of such wars and peace treaties, this too will come to naught. True peace will be attained only in an absolute concept of Brotherly Love and in the perception and conception that all mankind, as individuals or collectively, have their own way and right to live.

Back in 1945, the second great World War was brought to a sudden, dramatic and ghastly climax by the explosion of atom bombs over Japan. It can be said that these explosions ushered in a new atomic age. It can also be said that it is also an age of fear. Since that time, mankind all over the earth has walked in the shadow of that fear. Not only did the explosion of those atom bombs bring a new way and concept of life to our people, but it ushered in another age.

Almost immediately, the skies seemed to be filled with strange glowing objects, or spacecraft, from outer space. In the years following these various thousands of appearances, everyone has become space conscious. Every little boy has had a space suit. He can and does frequently indulge in rocket takeoffs and other things which are supposed to be part of this new Science while as yet man has not from this earth, produced a craft which is capable of traveling into free space.

As in the years following the first appearance of these craft, the world has been divided into two camps: those who do and those who do not, believe in flying saucers or spacecraft. In a certain sense both camps are right. The great mass and preponderance of evidence and photographs which support the appearance of many and numerous types of spacecraft cannot be denied nor can we deny the reasonable equations and views of those who do not believe. The truth is that spacecraft have not as yet appeared in this third dimensional world nor will they do so, for this third dimensional world or material world, as we know it, is not conducive to such craft and their operation.

In the preceding pages and chapters of this book,

much emphasis is given to what is termed space and energy, and the relationship of energy to mass. In the various equations and hypotheses which have, up until this time existed, all have missed certain relative and vital points in their relationship to energy and mass. It has not yet occurred to the scientist that while he has 101 elements and that they each express in their own way through the difference of their atomic structures a relative weight or a reactive consequence to certain known physical laws, if he thought for a moment it would become obvious that there were not only 101 elements but perhaps many thousands of other elements which existed in other dimensions which were not reactive to our physical laws.

He has also not correctly evaluated a true concept of an atom. An atom is not a solid particle, neither is it composed of a number of solid particles. An atom is composed of tiny vortexes of wave energies which are pulsating in outer rings of wave forms around a central vortex. This whole atomic structure is supported internally by what the scientist calls space. Actually, there is no such thing as space. Space is full; not with a solid substance or a static substance, but with a pulsating radiant energy. This energy comes from the Fountainhead or, as some people say, God. This energy which is constantly stemming from the Fountainhead, is also returning. It can therefore be said to be expanding and contracting simultaneously in all directions.

This Radiant Energy is Supremely Intelligent because It reflects the Infinite Mind of the Creative Fountainhead of God. Thus to be Infinite, it must express infinity and in infinity, it must become also finite. So therefore this Radiant Energy will express itself in countless dimensions and in countless forms. Thus it has done in our material world, in our

101 elements with which our scientists are familiar. We also know that these 101 elements are bound and held together in our world by certain physical laws, as they are called. These are gravity, inertia, momentum, centrifugal and centripetal force. There are other laws, of course, which are relative but of less consequence. These laws are the determining factors in the behavior of static masses of energy which you call elements.

The scientist has not yet become aware of the fact that, if we change the relationship of the emanating or sustaining life force of the atom, that it likewise changes its qualities and its relationship to the dynamic controlling forces. Many years ago the scientists were pondering about the sound barrier and thought that an aircraft could not pass through this supposed impregnable barrier.

Today, with many, many thousands of aircraft passing through this barrier, the scientist has learned certain facts, namely: that an airplane will behave quite differently after passing this certain line of demarcation which he calls the sound barrier. In other words, the known physical laws which govern the elements in his more familiar earth plane at stationary levels, have now somehow become altered after passing over this barrier.

In the future, the scientist will learn that in crossing over the ultimate barrier, which is the speed of light at 186,000 miles per second, he will have crossed the last known barrier which relates to his physical world. Between the sound barrier and the speed of light, however, he will find many other barriers or lines of demarcation—all of which change the relationship of mass and his elemental atomic structures to any of the known physical laws.

In the appearance of the various types of spacecraft, we have visualized that man on other planets has arrived at or past a point in his concept of science which relates to the ultimate barrier—the speed of light. Therefore, the appearance of any spacecraft in our third dimensional world is not an appearance in a true sense of energy and mass equated from our own standpoint or position. In other words, the scientist in the other world has succeeded in transmuting or levitating elemental atomic structures into a relationship with the energy source which takes it completely out of the realm of the known physical laws of this earth planet. He finds then that he is no longer affected by gravity, inertia, centrifugal force, or any other known factor. Actually, these laws are all one and the same. They are expressions of the cosmic energy as a controlling ingredient in the expression of energy as mass on our plane.

Therefore, it can be said that the appearance of a flying saucer to some individual, even though he may touch it or go for a ride in it, does not mean that he does this in a true physical sense. He has been, temporarily at least, transported in his concept to a point where he will somehow meet halfway with this spacecraft. The spacecraft itself has had to come down from a much more highly evolved position, into our lower earth strata.

We might compare these things with the chords of a piano. Thus while we are playing a chord at the high end of the scale, we can also play chords at the lower end of the scale which are either harmonious or inharmonious with our original basic chord.

The flying saucer man must therefore bring his craft down into a level of relationship which is closer to our known physical laws of the earth plane. This accounts for their peculiar behavior such as the wobbling or the pendulum-like motion, the tremendous rates of acceleration and their appearance of being glowing, white-hot, or transparent or translucent. Actually, these factors in themselves, are only relative to the plane which the saucer is in contact with at the moment. In its true state, it is not bound by our known physical laws. So you can see that spacecraft have not actually visited our world or our dimension, nor has anyone, in a true physical sense, ever contacted a spaceman or taken a ride in such a craft.

I can say this truly to those who have written books or accounts of these contacts: in reading all of the various stories of contacts which have been made by such persons, there always has been one important ingredient lacking. None of these people were, in themselves, a clairvoyant or a medium. In other words, they did not have the supersensitive development with which they could properly evaluate their position. Now, I know that the word clairvoyant is likely to arouse some antagonism or skepticism. Let me say, that if you have an open mind, you will start with Dr. Rhine of Duke University and when you thumb through all pages of history the past two or three thousand years, including the Bible, you will begin to understand what clairvoyance means. Clairvoyance is not some hocus-pocus thing which is practiced in some dark room. It is a clear-cut science which relates man with the higher and infinite source of his nature.

In the inward sense, every man is a part of God, as was pointed out by Christ. The very fact that we exist in material bodies supports this theory. We could not exist a single moment without the supporting force of the Infinite Mind of God, as He manifests himself in a continual stream of power, into every atom of our being. The very life of our body is dependent upon this source. Even the elements which we call food and take into our bodies are dependent, in their relationship to us, upon the expression of this cosmic force.

So in conclusion, may I say that man never will and cannot attain mastery over any dimension other than his own until he has mastered the concept that energy and mass, and the product of mass in relationship to energy, can be changed and altered. He must also learn that any or perhaps all of his present-day known physical laws will, in a few years, be discarded. Newton served his time; so did Einstein. There will be others who will come along and give a much newer and greater science; and with this new science, will come a new knowledge and a new wisdom which will more definitely relate the consciousness of man with his true, inner self. And with this consciousness that he is God, he will lay aside his warlike weapons. He will lay aside his desire and restlessness to conquer space. He will lay aside many of the aggressive militant attitudes which lack the common ingredient of brotherly love and thus he will come into his millennium, his Utopia.

It might be well to say that the announcement of the satellite might bring a new wave of appearance of spacecraft, and if you should see one of these, do not doubt what you have seen because it is quite likely that you have really seen it; but remember that this craft does not, in a true sense of the word, belong in your world. It does not react to our known physical laws simply because the minds who conceived that craft were definitely able to alter the relationship of the materials in that craft beyond the point where they were reactive to even such things as light. They have gone beyond the last of our known barriers or lines of demarcation. They have passed the point of 186,000 miles per second, which is the ultimate concept of our present-day scientists. Einstein tried to evaluate this by saying that such a relationship would assume a compressed effect as far as matter was concerned. He was not quite aware of the factor of frequency relationship with the infinite emanating Source of the Fountainhead. This is of the utmost consideration and importance. It will be the basis for the new world age and the new world science.

An announcement which recently came from one of our great medical centers, the Mayo Clinic, at Rochester, Minn., stated they had found that newly-born infants, just one day old, sometimes had the symptoms of cancer. There was no evidence in the report to indicate that such cancer symptoms were inherited, nor is there likely to be any. Another one of the great factors which man will have to learn and consider in relation to himself, is the factor of evolution and reincarnation.

In the pages of this book, you are told how you are a creature of many lives and many evolutions. You are continually revolving back through states of consciousness where you can learn to assimilate and evaluate certain concepts. After thousands of such evolutions, you will be objectively viewing God in an infinite number of aspects. And in such viewing, and in such knowledge, you will attain sufficient wisdom to assume mastery over these conditions. Thus, you will become one with God. As was explained, a person is not primarily a physical being, but a spiritual being; and he manifests into this world as a product of relationship with his spiritual self.

This spiritual self functions through his psychic body which links him with the supreme energizing force of the Fountainhead. This psychic body is composed of countless thousands of tiny vortexes, or wave forms, which can be similarized to atomic structures except, of course, they exist in a much higher dimension or frequency relationship. Many of our past occurrences and experiences in past lives are thus deeply imbedded in the intricate wave form patterns.

Cancer is a product of misalignment with the cosmic motivating force which sustains every atom in our body and, being nonproductive, becomes destructive in nature and, like many other diseases, multiplies its destructiveness. When the doctor or the psychiatrist, in this day and age or some future day and age, has properly assimilated this concept, he will be able to cure cancer. He will be able to cure many of the other diseases now incurable. He will have passed the last of the great barriers which have held civilization back in the slavery and drudgery of ignorance and disease.

So, friends, read this book through carefully. It was designed by the Great Ones themselves and these great intellects are much closer to God than you and I. It was brought into existence as an expression of Divine Love and the consciousness of these great Beings. And in reading, may you absorb the wisdom which is contained in its pages; and though you may or may not agree with all of the things which you read, you may rest assured that if you continue to pursue your course being inquisitive and open-minded, you will eventually understand all that is contained herein, and much more. It is quite obvious that with the great number of subjects which have been covered in this book, they necessarily had to be made quite brief. However, we have been promised a succession of similar books,* which will go into much more length and detail about the various subjects which have been covered primarily in these pages. But until this time, may you all rest in the graciousness of God's Love.

* Additional volumes of the Pulse of Creation series provide a continuity numbering five volumes: *The Voice of Eros, The Voice of Hermes, The Voice of Orion,* and *The Voice of Muse – Elysium – Unarius.*

TO THE READER

As this book goes to press, astronomers are becoming convinced of the possibility of life on other planets. The reader will be interested to know that no less an authority than Dr. Harlow Shapley has confirmed this in an interview with the press. We quote:

INTELLIGENT LIFE ON OTHER PLANETS CERTAIN, SAYS HARVARD ASTRONOMER

"A conclusion that living things with some kind of mentality exist in other worlds now is inevitable," says Dr. Harlow Shapley, noted Harvard University astronomer.

"Probably the conscious beings who inhabit other planet-like bodies in the universe are not like the earth's humans or manlike animals—the primates," Dr. Shapley told a lecture audience at the University of California. "Nevertheless, they must be capable of some kind of thinking," he said.

"The developments that make this conclusion inescapable," Dr. Shapley asserted, "are comparatively recent biological discoveries and they make a convincing picture when linked to findings in the fields of chemistry and astronomy.

"The biological findings include a mounting pile of evidence of a close relationship between molecules, viruses and genes. All things are made of molecules, which essentially are non-living aggregations of atoms.

The molecules which compose living organisms are made of carbon, oxygen, hydrogen, nitrogen and a few other chemicals.

"Scientists have found that viruses are elaborate molecules and they have some of the characteristics of living things. Under certain physical conditions, a non-living molecule accumulates more atoms and at some stage it takes on the aspects of a living organism. And genes, which are responsible for the transmission of heredity from one cell or one organism to a descendant, closely resemble viruses.

"On earth, it has taken a delicate balance of natural forces—just the right temperature range, a supply of water and air, and chemical conditions for bringing the atoms together to produce this," Dr. Shapley said. "And the findings of astronomers make it appear that conditions somewhat like those on earth must exist in countless other worlds."

— The Los Angeles Times, April 14, 1956.

NOTE

At present, mankind is entering into a space age and, in this advent, there is a great broadening in certain concepts and aspects concerning the possibilities of human life lived on other planets in other solar systems in our universe. While such a concession would have been ridiculed a few years ago, it is today a commonly accepted fact; and using the newly-developed radio telescopes, in conjunction with the already existing optical types, the man of science is probing the vast depths of space, trying to pick up any signals which would denote an intelligent race of humans on another planet.

This is the first of many steps the earthman will take before he succeeds in his quest to establish communication in some physical manner with other humans living on distant planets. As of today, the earthman scientist is not aware of the fact that communication between this and other planets has been going on for thousands of years. This has been done in three different ways. The first and more universally used method is mental communication; and every human who has been or is living is always—telepathically speaking—in direct communication with untold millions of humans living on uncounted numbers of distant planets.

The second and probably most important means of spiritual communication is spiritual transmigration. During every moment of earth's history, great numbers of discarnate entities (people without bodies), are traveling back and forth between various planets—some to be reborn in new physical bodies, others to influence through subconscious autosuggestion.

Third—there has also been in the past as well as the present, some interplanetary travel in certain kinds of spaceships. Considering the vast amount of interplanetary travel which has been and is going on, even though unseen and unrecognized by the material earthman, we can therefore safely present an obvious fact; that Unarius Channel, Dr. Norman, is an interplanetary traveler; but more than one who is motivated by some capricious whim. He is one of the original Lemurians, of which there were eleven, who came to this planet in a space-vehicle some 156,000 years ago and established the first Lemurian civilization. In this respect, he can remember and describe life on the planet Lemuria some 700 light years distant. Since that time, he has lived various periods of time in other and more closely associated planets such as Mars, Venus, Jupiter, etc., and is well-acquainted with many of the people who live there and can accurately describe their lives.

This Interplanetary Brotherhood method of communication, travel, etc., is part of the life contained in his works and again will be vindicated to some extent in future history. As Jesus said, "In my Father's house are many mansions."

The great and unending vistas of space contain not only material suns and solar systems, as they are known to the modern astronomers—but unseen and unknown existing in different vibratory rates as different dimensions are other vast and infinite reaches, all thickly populated with other kinds of planets composed from energy substances unknown to the earthman. These are the many mansions—places to be visited and lived in by any and all humans on their evolutionary pathway of life—reincarnation, if you please—but always a way in which the Infinite lives and regenerates.

To an old Lemurian Master-Scientist, the earth-man appears to be more puny, more elemental and more ridiculous than a group of primitive children playing a jungle game; yet he is temperate in his judgment—a temperance which has been born through vast millenniums of time—a wisdom acquired by consorting with the ageless and timeless inner dimensions which, like vast dervishes in an endless sea of time, gyrate in infinite numbers and convolutionary expressions, repeating each regeneration endlessly; for such is the way of the Infinite. A knowledge of this Infinite is yet to be acquired by the earthman which will supplant his archaic beliefs in demons and gods—an understanding which will relegate his religions back into the dust of his crumbling temples; a wisdom which will give him wings swifter than light —a way to span the vast regions of space in less than a twinkle of an eye; a high-road to eternity and a by-road into every man's heart.

Other Works by Ernest L. Norman

The Infinite Concept of Cosmic Creation
The Lesson Course—The Key to The Unarius Science

The Pulse of Creation Series

The Voice of Eros
The Voice of Hermes
The Voice of Orion
The Voice of Muse

Cosmic Continuum
Infinite Perspectus
Infinite Contact
Tempus Procedium
Tempus Invictus
Tempus Interludium Vols. I & II
The Truth About Mars
The Elysium (Parables)
The Anthinum (Poetry)

Also a publication now reprinted by
Unarius Publishing Company
The True Life of Jesus of Nazareth (1899)

The Sequel): The Story of the Little Red Box